TO WALK A
PAGAN
PATH

© Joan Stewart

ABOUT THE AUTHOR

Alaric Albertsson (Pennsylvania) is a founding member of Earendel Hearth, an Anglo-Saxon inhíred, and served in the 1990s as vice president and was on the board of directors of the Heartland Spiritual Alliance. He is currently a member of the Druidic organization Ár nDraíocht Féin (ADF) and serves as the Anglo-Saxon Vice Chieftain for the ADF Germanic kin, Eldr ok Iss.

Albertsson first embraced polytheism in the summer of 1971. At that time he had the opportunity to talk with rural people in the Ozark Mountains about traditional moon lore, weather lore, and folk beliefs and was strongly influenced by spiritist traditions. Over the past four decades, Albertsson's personal spiritual practice has developed as a synthesis of Anglo-Saxon tradition, country folklore, herbal studies, and rune lore.

TO WALK A

PAGAN

PATH

PRACTICAL SPIRITUALITY
FOR EVERY DAY

ALARIC ALBERTSSON

Llewellyn Publications
Woodbury, Minnesota

First Edition
First Printing, 2013

Book design by Donna Burch
Cover art: iStockphoto.com/22804521/Loradora, 8168792/Jamie Farrant,
        17975826/Alonzo Design, 6098770/SpiffyJ
Cover design by Kevin R. Brown
Editing by Andrea NefInterior art by Llewellyn Art Department

Llewellyn Publications is a registered trademark of Llewellyn Worldwide, Ltd.

Library of Congress Cataloging-in-Publication Data
Albertsson, Alaric.
  To walk a pagan path : practical spirituality for every day / by Alaric
Albertsson. — First Edition.
      pages   cm
  Includes bibliographical references and index.
  ISBN 978-0-7387-3724-9
  1. Neopaganism. I. Title.
  BP605.N46A43 2013
  299'.94—dc23
                                                                2013027481

Llewellyn Worldwide does not participate in, endorse, or have any authority or responsibility concerning private business transactions between our authors and the public.
  All mail addressed to the author is forwarded, but the publisher cannot, unless specifically instructed by the author, give out an address or phone number.
  Any Internet references contained in this work are current at publication time, but the publisher cannot guarantee that a specific location will continue to be maintained. Please refer to the publisher's website for links to authors' websites and other sources.

Llewellyn Publications
A Division of Llewellyn Worldwide, Ltd.
2143 Wooddale Drive
Woodbury, MN 55125-2989
www.llewellyn.com

Printed in the United States of America

DEDICATION
For Alene.

ACKNOWLEDGMENTS

This book explores personal experiences, both my own and those of other Pagan men and women, and therefore leaves me with countless people whom I owe thanks to. I feel that I should first thank the many people who midwived our contemporary culture, people like Gerald Gardner, Sybil Leek, Paul Huson, Zsuzsanna Budapest, Oberon Zell, Raymond Buckland, Leo Martello, and others. I could not possibly name them all. They laid the groundwork for what would eventually expand into the extensive and diverse Pagan communities we have today.

I also need to thank the people whom I've quoted, such as Ian Corrigan and M. Cassius Julianus. Special thanks to those who agreed to be interviewed for this book: Mario Munive, Diane Dahm, Irisa MacKenzie, Joy and Jack Bennett, Devin Hunter, and Nick Egelhoff. In sharing their own experiences, they have each brought something special to this book.

Finally, I would like to thank my editors, Elysia Gallo and Andrea Neff, for their invaluable help. I don't think any writer actually enjoys the editorial process, but both of my editors caught errors that would have embarrassed me grievously had those errors gone to print. I was blessed to have the opportunity to work with these two wonderful women.

CONTENTS

INTRODUCTION

This is a book about something most Pagans aspire to do; it is about expressing our spirituality in our daily lives. After your coven meeting comes to a close or your grove ritual ends, how do you continue to live as a Pagan from day to day?

Years ago a non-Pagan friend said to me, "I know why you're always so happy, Alaric. It's all the holidays you Pagans have. You have Christmas all year long!"

There was a kernel of truth in that thought. For the majority of us Pagans who observe the Wheel of the Year, another holiday celebration comes approximately every six weeks. We barely have time to put away the spring equinox decorations before we start planning for our Beltane celebrations, and then Midsummer and then Lammas. Depending on your path or tradition, some of these holidays will have more significance than others, but the celebratory spirit flows through our lives like a spiraling stream without end.

We can find even more fulfillment by expanding our spiritual expression beyond these seasonal observances and into our daily lives. But to live fully as a Pagan requires intentional effort, and usually a little planning. The good news is that the rewards far outweigh the effort.

Think of this book as a tool kit for building a Pagan life. The book provides some tools, but the design of your life will depend on your path or tradition, your personal needs, and all of the many factors that have made you a unique individual. Some of the ideas you'll find herein will be more useful than others. Some you may eschew altogether.

For example, in the book I suggest beekeeping as one means of building a connection with the earth, but this may be inappropriate if you are allergic to bee venom, suffer from entomophobia (fear of insects), or do not have the funds for the initial start-up expenses. Beekeeping is not for everybody.

Depending on your life design, some of the ideas presented here may be useful, but only after they have been altered for your own use. As far as possible I have tried to be inclusive of the vast diversity of Pagan beliefs, traditions, and experiences, but feel free to adapt anything given within these pages to fit your own needs. *To Walk a Pagan Path* is about expressing *your* spirituality in your daily life!

My own path is Saxon, as you already know if you have read other books that I have written. The inspiration that shapes my spirituality comes from the culture and traditions of pre-Christian England, so this book has a lot of examples from a Saxon viewpoint. However, the ideas behind those examples can and should be personalized to reflect your own tradition. Whether your path is Wiccan, Saxon, Celtic, Hellenic, Kemetic, Ásatrú, or some other tradition, this book will help you expand your spirituality into a more fulfilling lifestyle.

In the first chapter I'll tell you about seven things you can do to really integrate Paganism into your everyday life in a meaningful way. You very likely do some of these things already. Most are steps you can take over the next couple weeks to expand your spiritual experience. As with everything else in this book, all seven steps can be easily personalized for your own spiritual tradition.

Most of the seven steps require little explanation, but the second and third chapters will explore the purpose and methods of creating sacred time. In the second chapter we will look at personalizing the sacral calendar, and in the third chapter I discuss expressing your spirituality through your daily rituals.

In the remainder of the book we will explore different activities to help strengthen your connection with the earth. Again, some of these activities may be inappropriate for your lifestyle, and some may need to be tweaked or personalized, but some may eventually become cherished traditions for you exactly as they are presented here. These later chapters explore the possibilities of expanding your spiritual experience by working with companion animals, growing some of your own food, connecting with trees and wildlife, keeping hens or honeybees, baking bread, making your own incenses and candles, and more.

You may find that you derive enjoyment and spiritual enrichment from most of the activities in *To Walk a Pagan Path*. Many of these can be integrated into your life as seasonal projects either for you alone or for group activities. Your coven may decide to make ritual candles every Imbolc (as some of my Wiccan friends do), blend incenses at Midsummer, and bake bread at Lughnasadh. In this way you can enjoy a lot of these projects without them overwhelming your life.

Or you may find yourself drawn to one specific activity, and that is okay too. More than one Pagan has discovered a lifelong interest in herb magic after growing a few pots of basil and sage! Developing your personal sacral calendar and daily devotions could lead you to explore your spirituality in ways you have not yet imagined. That is the wonderful thing about walking a Pagan path: we are never quite sure where it will take us, but the journey is always interesting.

SEVEN STEPS TO A NEW WAY OF LIVING

How do you express your spirituality from day to day?

The customs and spiritual practices of the early, pre-Christian Pagan cultures were passed down from one generation to the next. These old ways were traditions for respecting and interacting with the gods and other spirit denizens, and they varied from one culture to another. The Anglo-Saxon, for example, gave due offerings before a wéoh, which was an image or symbol of the honored deity. The early Roman honored his family's numina (guardian spirits) at a household lararium, an object often resembling a small cupboard, which served as a home for those spirits. The early Greek began every ritual with an offering to the goddess Hestia. Each culture had its own customs. Many Paleo-Pagans—whether Greek, Roman, or Saxon—were undoubtedly passionate and sincere in their piety, but their spiritual paths were largely a matter of circumstance rather than choice. The Celt and the Egyptian, the Saxon and the Greek, they all observed their respective customs because those were the only customs they were familiar and comfortable with.

By contrast, contemporary Pagans—almost without exception—intentionally choose the paths we follow. This is necessarily true for the "first-generation Pagan," who was not raised as a Pagan, but in today's multicultural environment even children born into polytheistic households are usually encouraged to explore and appreciate other spiritual paths and to choose their own paths with knowledge and intention. Today's Pagan—whether raised in a Pagan home or not—makes a conscious decision about his or her personal spiritual journey.

This intentional choice may be one of the most significant distinctions between contemporary Pagans and our Paleo-Pagan ancestors. We have expectations of our spiritual paths. For the majority of today's Pagans this includes the expectation of a connection between us and the earth, so much so that Pagan spirituality has often been labeled "earth religion" or "earth-based religion." Our ancestors had no need to reconnect with the earth; they were immersed in its whims and tides. In the pre-industrial world, the rural population was much greater than it is today. Urban centers like Rome and Athens were few and far between, and even in those ancient cities the residents were far more directly affected by the earth's mood swings.

Today, in developed nations at least, we need not fear starvation if the local grain crop fails. For the majority of us, severe winter weather only means a higher than usual utility bill. We are still dependent on the earth, but not as directly as our ancestors were, and for the most part this is a good thing. Nevertheless, we have lost something in the process, and it is this disconnection from the natural world that has inspired many people to explore "earth-based" Pagan spirituality.

Because of this intentional spirituality, Pagans today often attempt to follow what the early Saxons might have called *Hal Sidu*, meaning healthy or holistic traditions. Hal Sidu engages and integrates all parts of the self. Exactly how many parts there are depends on one's spiritual paradigm. As a Saxon Pagan, I expect Hal Sidu to engage my rational thought, stimulate my memories and emotion, arouse my source of inspiration, balance my physical body, and fortify my identity. In the Saxon tradition, these are all equally important parts of the "self." Pagans who follow other paths will have other definitions of the self, of course. For the sake of simplicity, let us make use of a popular contemporary paradigm and define Hal Sidu as the integration of body, mind, and spirit.

I use the Old English term Hal Sidu for intentional Pagan spirituality because I follow a Saxon path, but a Roman Pagan might call it the Vetera Valens ("worthy traditions"). An Icelandic Pagan could call it Heildræn Venjur ("holistic habits"). The name is not important. By any name, intentional Pagan spirituality helps us reconnect with the earth and integrate all parts of the self into one whole being.

Hal Sidu—or whatever term you prefer—is not a matter of belief. In fact, "belief" is relatively unimportant in polytheistic religions. Yes, the Paleo-Pagans believed in their gods, but it was in the way modern people believe in gravity or electricity, not in the way a child believes in the Tooth Fairy. When we apply the logic that we apply to every other aspect of the human experience to our perception of the divine, it is patently obvious that the gods are real. We can conclude that the goddess Athena is real, for example, because she has spoken to and interacted with thousands of people over thousands of years—and she is no "less real" just because Bob decides, for whatever reason, not to believe in her existence. Early Pagans knew the gods were real; for them it was not an issue of personal belief.

What matters to the polytheist are not people's beliefs, but people's actions—their words and deeds. Traditional Pagan spirituality is *orthopraxic*, focusing on shared practices and traditions rather than beliefs. This remains true even today in Pagan paths such as British Traditional Witchcraft, in most forms of polytheistic Reconstructionism, and for the international Neo-Pagan fellowship Ár nDraíocht Féin. It is your actions that define you and shape the world around you. And as with all other things, it is by your actions that you integrate body, mind, and spirit. Not by thinking about it. Not by talking about it. It is something you do.

When we take no action toward developing an intentional Pagan spirituality, it is often because we do not know where to begin rather than from a lack of desire. Few books address this issue of how to live as a Pagan after closing the ritual and washing up the chalice or mead horn. Many Pagans, especially those new to polytheism, are unsure how to reach out and touch the earth both physically and spiritually.

Hal Sidu—holistic custom—demands that we do this very thing; that we touch the earth, taking action to build a personal Pagan lifestyle. How you accomplish this will be a reflection of your own interests, needs, and circumstances. The important thing is not the approach you take—which will vary from one person to another—but that you do *something*, some little thing each day to connect with your gods and with the world around you.

There are many ways to do this. You might find a connection through rituals that sacralize your daily activities, or by mindfully working with a familiar. You might find it by literally touching the earth, armed with a spade and a hoe, raising some of your own food and actively participating in the eternal cycle of receiving and giving back. Or maybe you will find more inspiration in crafting your own ritual candles and incense. Whatever the means, building an intentional, personal Pagan lifestyle will help you integrate body, mind, and spirit into something whole and complete.

DEDICATION RITE

When making any long-term change in your life, it can help to begin by formally dedicating yourself to the work. This is true for almost any change: beginning a diet, giving up a bad habit, or learning a new language or skill. It is also true for those who wish to develop an intentional Pagan lifestyle.

We have discussed how Hal Sidu demands action, so why not take action right now? If you would like to make changes in your life to integrate body, mind, and spirit, read the following description of the Dedication Rite and then perform the ritual yourself.

No, really. Do it now.

Of course this assumes that you are in or near some private place where you can perform a rite without attracting undue attention. If you are reading this at a public library or while riding a city bus, you should probably wait for a more opportune time. Otherwise, if you have reasonable privacy, what are you waiting for? You may not know yet exactly how you want to practice Hal Sidu, but you can take this initial action, dedicating yourself to the work, nevertheless. Think of it as your first step toward a new way of living. The rite is short and simple, and requires minimal equipment. All you need is a candle and something to give as an offering, which can be incense, wine or mead to pour as a libation, or almost anything else that seems appropriate to you. The candle can be paraffin or beeswax, and can be any color you happen to have readily available.

Of course you may tweak or expand the Dedication Rite to suit your spiritual needs. If you have a personal relationship with a particular deity, you might place a statue or symbol of that deity next to the candle. If you are Wiccan, you might want to cast a circle as a part of the rite. Your choice of an offering will likely be influenced by your spiritual orientation. As a Saxon Pagan, my first choice would be to pour a libation of mead. A Roman Pagan might instead offer a libation of olive oil, while a Greek Pagan might choose to burn sweet herbs on a charcoal disk.

The wording of the rite may also be altered to reflect your needs and spiritual orientation. What is given here should be taken as a suggestion; it is not a magical formula.

Set your candle and anything else you might need on your *myse*, or working surface. If you have been Pagan for a long time, this will very likely be your household altar. If you do not have an altar or other consecrated working surface, any clean, level surface will suffice—for now, at least. Later in this chapter we will discuss why it is important to have sacred space—an altar, by whatever name you call it—at some place in your home.

Take a few slow, deep breaths to relax and prepare yourself mentally. Then light the candle as you say:

Spirits who live in this place,
ancestors who have brought me to this place,
gods and goddesses who bless this place,
know that you are remembered and bear witness to this rite.

Again, take a few slow, deep breaths. Try to feel the presence of the spirits around you. It does not matter whether you feel, see, or hear anything. Very often the adage "No news is good news" holds true when interacting with the spirit world. Our contemporary Pagan culture tends to overemphasize magic, and I have known some people who felt there was something wrong because they were not receiving vivid psychic impressions whenever they paused to listen for their gods, their ancestors, or local spirits. However, this was more likely because they were doing fine; there was no reason for spirits to advise or admonish them. You may or may not receive any impressions, but give the spirits the opportunity to respond before proceeding.

Now give your offering. You may use an offering bowl if you are holding the rite indoors and have a libation or a food offering. Such an offering should be poured or placed on the earth at the earliest opportunity after the conclusion of the rite. Offerings of incense should be burned. After making the offering, say:

Accept this offering, freely given with my love and respect.
I come before you and declare my intention

to live more fully as a Pagan,
to take action each day that will attune me to the universe.
I ask for your guidance in my choices,
that through my words and deeds
I might bring honor to the old gods,
bring pride to my ancestors
and bring beauty and well-being into the world around me.
Let my actions keep me mindful of the earth,
from which I was born and to which I will someday return.
So shall I thank you with joy and gratitude.

Since you have asked for the spirits' guidance, a few more moments of silence while you listen to them is appropriate. Then end the rite by extinguishing the candle and saying "So mote it be" or "Ic bedde éow nu" or whatever you would ordinarily say when concluding a rite. If you are new to Pagan ways and have not yet chosen a path, "So mote it be" will do fine.

SEVEN STEPS
TO A PAGAN PRACTICE

For many people who are new to Pagan ways, the variety of paths and practices can be overwhelming. It can be difficult to know where you should even begin. A few years ago I attended a presentation given by Ian Corrigan on developing a personal Pagan practice. Corrigan is a former Archdruid of the international Pagan organization Ár nDraíocht Féin. Inspired by his ideas, I developed my own "seven step program" to help the new Pagan get his or her bearings. The seven steps are not intended to lead you to any particular Pagan path, but rather to help you find whatever path is right for you. Even if you were born into a Pagan family or chose a Pagan path years ago, you may find something of value in these seven steps.

Step 1: Connecting with Spirit

You have already made at least one ephemeral connection with Spirit, assuming you have performed the Dedication Rite. We connect with Spirit whenever we ask for guidance or bring gifts (offerings).

This first step is where people new to Pagan traditions can find themselves bewildered by the seemingly endless possible paths to choose from. There are so many gods and goddesses, from so many pantheons! Where does a person begin? It may be that a deity has already connected with you. People who have had this experience will often say, "She called me" or "He tapped me on the shoulder," but this is the exception rather than the rule. It is far more likely that you will need to make the initial gesture. First you must decide which god or goddess you would like to make a connection with, and to do this you should find a pantheon that feels comfortable to you.

A pantheon is a cultural "family" of gods and goddesses. The Hellenic (Greek) pantheon includes the twelve gods and goddesses of the Dodekatheon: Zeus, Hera, Apollo, Athena, and so on. The Saxon pantheon includes Woden, Frige, Thunor, and Eostre, among others. The Irish pantheon includes deities such as Brigid and Manannán mac Lir. The gods and goddesses within any given pantheon have well-defined relationships with each other.

No one pantheon is better than another, so how do you choose? One thing to consider is your own lineage. If you come from an Italian background, the Roman pantheon might be a good choice. If your name is O'Reilly, the Irish pantheon could be the right pantheon for you. Of course you are not constrained by your background in any way, which is a good thing since very few of us in the United States today are descended from a single cultural lineage.

If a particular pantheon just feels right to you, then by all means go with that feeling. Maybe you were inspired by Greek mythology when you were in school. Maybe the comic book version of Thor (who shares little other than his name with the real Thor) has kindled your interest in the Norse gods of Asgard. There are infinite reasons why you might be drawn to a pantheon. Most of those reasons may seem to be nothing more than random chance, but I have found that random chance very often has some underlying purpose.

If neither your lineage nor your heart leads you to a path, go to your local library and check out books on several mythologies. I dislike the word *mythology* because of its secondary definition meaning "something untrue." *Myth* is a Greek word that simply means "story," and mythologies are collections of ancient stories explaining the order of the universe or a society's ideals and customs. With this in mind, look through the mythology books you have checked out and familiarize yourself with them.

Then pick something.

When it comes to choosing a pantheon, as with all other things, take action. Do not worry whether or not you have chosen the right pantheon, because there is no right or wrong answer to this. Whichever pantheon appeals to you the most *right now* is the best pantheon for you *right now*. Just as a tentative first date could eventually lead to marriage, your initial choice of a pantheon may lead to a lifetime commitment, but you can change pantheons later if you find that your first choice was not the best choice for you.

After choosing a pantheon, your next action should be to decide on a god or goddess to connect with. This choice usually depends on your own personal interests, as you are more likely to establish a good connection with a deity who shares those interests. A Kemetic (Egyptian) Pagan who has five cats and an extensive collection of cat statuettes would do well to connect with the cat-headed goddess Bast. A Saxon Pagan working in the field of law enforcement might connect with Tiw, a god of order and justice. A Roman Pagan who appreciates fine wines could establish an initial connection with Bacchus. But if you find that a god or goddess in the pantheon just feels right to you, even if you are not sure why, go with the feeling.

Find a private, safe place where you can connect with the deity. This will probably be at your household altar, if you have one, but the important thing is that you find a location where you will be undisturbed. Bring a gift, an offering, with you to establish a cycle of reciprocity with the deity. The choice of an offering will depend on the pantheon and the deity. If you are unsure of what to offer, mead (honey wine) is usually appreciated by most northern European deities, while olive oil is usually appreciated by the gods and goddesses of southern Europe. Other cultures have their own preferences, but be sure to bring something. Any gift is better than no gift at all!

If you are indoors, you will need an offering bowl. Pour a libation (liquid offering) into the bowl as you address the deity. Afterward, when it is convenient, take the bowl outside and pour the libation out directly onto the earth. Solid offerings, especially food, may also be symbolically placed in the offering bowl and then later set out on or buried in the earth.

Somebody once asked me why I bother with an offering, since a god can presumably obtain almost anything he desires. This is like belittling a handcrafted present that a child makes for a parent. Of course the parent could have made or purchased something much nicer, but he or she will be delighted with the gift nevertheless. It is the act of giving that is appreciated, and the worth of the gift is directly proportionate to the effort put into it.

When you are ready to approach the deity and give your offering, the words should be your own, coming from your heart rather than from the pages of a book. First, greet the deity by name, give your offering, and ask that it be accepted. If you are indoors, pour or place the offering into your offering bowl. If you are outdoors, place the offering directly onto the earth. The exception to this is the offering that is burned, usually a pleasant incense. You can use incense cones or sticks, but I think a personal blend of aromatic herbs is more meaningful. These are burned in a censer over charcoal disks that can be purchased at almost any New Age or religious supply shop.

After giving your offering, introduce yourself and ask for the deity's guidance and blessing. This is not the time to make any specific requests. Later on you may ask for favors, after you have established a mutual relationship, but at this point you are simply acknowledging a willingness to accept whatever blessings the deity may offer.

Next comes the most important part: listening. Quiet yourself as much as possible and be mindful of any impressions you may have. The response of the god or goddess rarely manifests as an audible voice, although that can occasionally happen. You may have a fleeting vision, or smell an odor that evokes a long-forgotten memory. Or you may experience a "knowing," a sudden awareness of the deity's presence and message to you.

Or you may experience nothing at all.

Do not be discouraged if this is the case. You are not going to have a supernal experience every time you reach out to the gods and spirits. In giving an offering to the deity, you have taken an action and made a connection. If you still feel no reciprocal connections after two or three more "visits" with the deity, politely move on to another god or goddess.

There are many Pagans today who take a more scattered, eclectic approach to connecting with Spirit, leaping from one pantheon to another, collecting "patron" deities as if they were Hummel figurines. Imagine yourself walking down a sidewalk in Manhattan, greeting everyone you pass. How deep is your relationship with these passersby? You are not investing a significant amount of time with any individual person. You do not really know any of them. In the same way, it can be difficult to develop truly meaningful relationships with a dozen gods and goddesses gathered from unrelated pantheons. I do not recommend this approach at all. If you want to become good friends with somebody, you spend a lot of time with that person. You meet his or her family and friends. Likewise, if you want a good relationship with a god or goddess, you should devote a lot of time to that deity.

Of course, the gods are not the only manifestations of Spirit. You may also wish to connect with your ancestral spirits, following a similar process of giving an offering and then opening yourself to the blessings of your ancestors. By ancestors I mean not only blood ancestors, but also those who have inspired you in some way. In Saxon tradition, as with all Germanic paths, reverence for one's ancestors is very important. Indeed, ancestor reverence is an important aspect of most Pagan traditions. Ancestral spirits have a vested interest in you—you are their heritage—and so they are more disposed to offer you aid and counsel.

Another connection to make is with the local spirits. Depending on your spiritual focus, you may know these as fairies, elves, nymphs, or by some other name. These spirits are your neighbors, and, like mortal neighbors, they can aid or hinder you. Thus it is to your benefit to foster good relationships with them. If you practice Hal Sidu, you will almost certainly find yourself interacting with your spirit neighbors. When you engage in activities that touch the earth in some way—planting a seed, trimming back an unruly bush, weeding the garden—remember to offer a bit of cornmeal or wine to the local spirits. Then pause for a moment and listen. They might have something to share with you.

Whatever your approach—whether you are more comfortable approaching a deity, or your ancestors or local entities—the first and most essential step toward living as a Pagan is to connect in some way with Spirit.

Step 2: Creating Sacred Space

"Either the gods have a place in one's home, or they do not."

So says Marcus Cassius Iulianus, a contemporary Roman Pagan and founder of the Reconstructionist organization Nova Roma. He was speaking of the household altar, and I completely agree.

Once you have made a connection with Spirit, your next action should be to establish a place where you can maintain and continue to build that connection. This can be as simple or as elaborate as you wish, but there should be some place in your home that is sacred and set aside for your gods.

The design of this sacred space will depend on several factors. The first factor to consider is your spiritual focus. A Greek altar will always have a flame, even if this is only a single candle. A Saxon altar (wéofod) will always have a statue or symbolic image (wéoh) of the honored deity. Whatever path you have chosen, your altar should be a reflection of its aesthetics. The sacred space you reserve for your gods should be a space where they can rest comfortably.

Where you live will also influence the design of your sacred space. Some Pagans devote entire rooms to their worship, furnished with appropriate wall hangings, cabinets for incense and regalia, and the altar itself. This obviously is not an option if you are renting a studio apartment, nor is it necessarily the best choice even if you do have that option. For one person, a separate room may be a place of wonder and enchantment; for another, it may be a room that is easily forgotten amidst the distractions of daily life.

My own household altar is in the living room, so I pass by it constantly. This works best for me. The altar itself is a library table. This gives me plenty of space and fits the room, which is fairly large. In theory, I could have the same altar in a studio apartment, but it would be overwhelming and unattractive. Consider the surrounding environment, and keep in mind that bigger is not always better.

Another factor is how "out" you are as a Pagan. Nobody looking at my household altar—with its idols and runes and offering bowl—is going to mistake me for a Southern Baptist. But many people, because of fear or circumstance, do not have this freedom. Sadly, even in the twenty-first century, some of us could lose our jobs if our spirituality became common knowledge due to the ignorance and prejudice of others. Others are simply afraid of censure by friends, neighbors, or relatives.

If this presents a problem for you, there are two possible solutions. The first is to locate your altar where it will not be seen by others. You could set up the altar in your bedroom or even in a basement. This is where a separate room becomes practical if you have a large house. Keep in mind that somebody may discover your altar no matter how careful you are. And this really is a problem, then, because the altar was hidden, which implies that you have something to be ashamed about.

A better solution is to "hide" the altar in plain sight. Your altar can be subtle and unassuming, appearing to the uninitiated as nothing more than a table with a couple of knick-knacks. A Saxon Pagan, for example, could arrange a small table with a single, attractive candle, a large quartz crystal (representing the god Thunor), and a ceramic (offering) bowl. While it is better, of course, if you can be out and open about your spirituality, the important thing is that you have sacred space where you can connect with Spirit undisturbed.

Your primary household altar should be indoors so you can approach your gods even in the most inclement weather. But if you have the resources, by all means, touch the earth! A secondary, outdoor altar will give you the opportunity to listen to the wind, enjoy the warmth of the sun against your skin, and feel the rich soil beneath you. Like your primary altar, an outdoor altar can be as simple or elaborate as you wish. When I moved to Pennsylvania, I bought a house with a gazebo in the back garden. From the beginning, I knew there would be very little "sit in the gazebo" time. Does anybody today really spend much time in a gazebo? Rather than let it sit empty and useless, I converted the gazebo into a *wéofodsteall*, a Saxon shrine, dedicated to the god Ing Fréa. Following Anglo-Saxon tradition, I placed an image representing Ing Fréa inside the gazebo. (The Old English word for an altar, *wéofod*, literally means "the place where the image of the deity stands.") I placed a few decorative stones around this image just to make it attractive. Then I planted herbs and flowers around the gazebo, because Ing is the Lord of the Elves and governs green growing things.

But an outdoor altar can be as simple as a flat stone set in a place where you feel especially close to your gods, along with the minimal requirements, if any, of your spiritual path.

So far we have looked at the altar as sacred space for our gods. Some people, myself included, like to maintain a separate altar to honor their ancestors. This is not strictly necessary; however, we tend to approach our ancestors in a different way than we approach deities. As one Pagan recently described it to me, going to your deities with a problem is like seeking an audience with the king, whereas going to your ancestors is like asking help from your family.

An ancestral altar can include photographs of ancestors you knew in life, as well as symbolic representations of more distant ancestors. I have known some Pagans who made ancestor "dolls" sculpted from clay or sewn as stuffed poppets. Some of these dolls were intended to represent specific ancestors, while others were more symbolic. The ancestral altar might also hold items that were significant to one or more of your ancestors. My grandfather's fishing knife rests on my own ancestral altar, next to a photograph of him. An incense burner and offering bowl on the altar will serve to receive the gifts you bring to your ancestors.

As I mentioned earlier, ancestors are not necessarily limited to your biological lineage. I define ancestors as those who have, in some way or another, shaped us and brought us to where we are today. An adopted parent (and that person's parents) is an ancestor. If you are widowed, your spouse is an ancestor. A teacher or older neighbor who inspired you as a child is an ancestor. A close friend who shaped your life significantly before he or she passed away could be considered an ancestor. Even a beloved pet might be an ancestor, for we rely on our companion animals today to a degree that people previously did not.

I do honor the companion animals with whom I have shared my life, but not at the same altar where I honor my human ancestors. Again, this is because I have a different relationship with them. I might commune with my dog Sheena for comfort, but I am not likely to go to her for advice, as brilliant as she was.

Not everyone has the space for multiple altars, and not everyone feels the need for this. However, you should have at least one sacred space somewhere in your home where you can connect with Spirit. Do the gods and ancestors have a place in your home, or do they not?

Step 3: Creating Sacred Time

If you do nothing with your altar, it is not truly an altar; it is merely a table or shelf holding an incense burner, a couple of candles, and perhaps two or three interesting statuettes. The activities that take place at that table or shelf—the reverence, the offerings, and the meditation—are what give meaning to your sacred space. Therefore your next action should be to set aside sacred time to connect with Spirit consistently.

The value of this step cannot be overemphasized. Life happens to all of us. You may have an important test coming up, or your boss has asked you to work overtime, or the baby has kept you up all night. These things happen, and when they do, it is easy to put your spiritual needs and obligations aside "until tomorrow." The problem is, tomorrow is always a day away, because life continues to happen constantly. Next week you may have the flu or a surprise visit from an old friend. The week following that will bring its own demands. Those perfect, serene moments when you can connect with Spirit without interruption are rare unless you take action to create them yourself.

Consistency is the key. People who are successful in any endeavor have made a habit of actions that lead to their success. They act consistently. A crash diet will not lead to long-term weight control. People who succeed in weight loss have developed consistent, healthy eating habits. Likewise, you cannot have a well-trained dog simply by taking it to a series of ten obedience classes. Well-behaved dogs have owners who consistently reward their good choices and ignore their bad choices. Successful artists paint or draw consistently, successful writers write consistently, and successful athletes exercise consistently. Habitual behavior keeps us focused on our goals.

To develop a habit of connecting with Spirit, set aside a specific time for doing this. You are setting aside sacred time for yourself, your gods, and your ancestors. Find a time in your schedule that you can devote to this. You devote time every day to your physical body: bathing or showering, brushing your teeth, preparing meals. You perform these actions consistently, and it is no more difficult to set aside a consistent time devoted to your spiritual body. When you create sacred time, you begin developing a habitual, empowering behavior that will nurture your relationship with your gods and ancestors.

Consistency requires a realistic goal on your part. Let's go back to the example of training a dog. My own dogs are relatively well behaved because I work with them, consistently, every day. Do we have an hour-long session of obedience work? Of course not. Professional trainers of animal actors can devote themselves to long, daily lessons, but most of us, including me, cannot consistently have daily, hour-long training sessions. Instead, Lucky and Caesar wait patiently while I fill their food bowls, sit at the back door until I tell them they can go out, and, once a day, every day, we quickly run through a set of activities: sit, down, stay, give me your paw, stand, go do the dishes. (Okay, neither Lucky nor Caesar will wash the dishes. I am still working on that.) They practice what they know in short intervals. I can be consistent because I keep it short.

If your goal is to give an offering to Woden and then meditate for thirty minutes every evening, you will almost surely fail. Your sacred time should define the *minimal* time you will invest in connecting with Spirit. You are not limited to this. When the circumstances are right and you feel the need, you absolutely can give an offering to Woden every evening and then meditate for thirty minutes. But be honest with yourself and acknowledge that this is not something that you can do indefinitely. Setting aside sacred time is a long-term habit, something that will eventually be as essential and natural as putting on your underwear in the morning (assuming it is your habit to wear underwear).

How much time can you give to your gods and ancestors consistently? How much time can you fit into your life, not just today or this week, but for years to come?

A commitment of fifteen minutes every week is not unreasonable. Does this sound ridiculously simple? It should, because a ridiculously simple commitment is a commitment you are likely to stick with. Choose a day and a time when you will spend at least fifteen minutes at your altar, giving offerings to Spirit and listening to what your gods and ancestors may have to say. The day and time should fit your lifestyle. One person may find it easiest and most natural to commit to fifteen minutes every Tuesday evening, while Saturday mornings may be more suitable for another.

Exactly what you do during those fifteen minutes should reflect your spirituality. Some offering should be given to Spirit to nurture the process of reciprocity. We give to our gods and our ancestors so that they might give to us in return. The offering may be as simple as a pinch of incense. Norse and Saxon Pagans will probably offer libations of mead or ale. A Roman Pagan may offer spelt, a grain related to wheat that is often sold in health food stores. Traditional offerings for the Egyptian Pagan include bread and beer. After giving the offering, the remainder of your fifteen minutes can be spent in prayer, in singing or chanting, in meditation, or in any other activity that connects you with Spirit.

You might find yourself doing this every day, and spending half an hour or more at your altar rather than just fifteen minutes. However, when life becomes complicated, you should strive to the best of your ability to honor the sacred time—those fifteen minutes each week—that you have set aside for your gods and your ancestors. By creating sacred time, you ensure that your spirituality remains a part of your routine throughout the most chaotic periods of your life.

However simple this commitment may seem, there may be an occasional week when even that is impossible. You may have to make a sudden trip to the emergency room, either for yourself or for somebody else. Or you discover that your basement has flooded. There are things that can disrupt even the easiest commitment. When something like this happens, attend to the problem but make your sacred time the next highest priority. If you put it off any longer than absolutely necessary, you diminish its worth.

Step 4: Sacralize Daily Activities

You have connected with your gods and your ancestors. You have created a sacred space—an altar—where you can approach them, and have set aside sacred time to do so. When you have done all of this, the time has come for your next action, which is to expand your spiritual awareness beyond the altar and more fully into your life.

This is the goal of Hal Sidu. Holistic tradition entreats us to integrate our spirituality with the rest of our lives. Just as your physical body is sustained by the air you take into your lungs throughout the day, so is your spiritual body sustained by the mindful actions you take to sacralize your daily activities. These simple actions will help you connect with Spirit from the moment you awaken until you go to sleep at night.

The third chapter of this book is devoted to the daily rituals that every Pagan can use to integrate his or her spirituality into a daily routine. Your personal routine, however, is unique to yourself, and for this reason you should strive to develop unique ways to sacralize the activities in your own life. Hopefully the suggestions in the third chapter will inspire you to do just that.

As a writer, for example, I spend much of my day sitting at my computer. More often than not, this routine begins with a fresh cup of coffee. The coffee helps wake up my body, and the act of writing itself stimulates my mind, but what of my spirit? I want to bring my entire being into the process of writing,

to integrate my body, mind and spirit. To do this, I set aside a
moment for prayer, saying:

> *Woden, World Wanderer,*
> *let my words be true,*
> *that they might bring honor to my folk*
> *and to the elder ways.*
> *Ic bidde the nu.*

The last line is pronounced "eech biddeh they noo" and is
Old English for "I ask you now." Woden, if you are not famil-
iar with Saxon tradition, is a god of inspiration and magic.
His name gave us our word for the fourth day of the week,
Wednesday (Woden's Day).

You can see here how this little ritual is unique to my own
daily routine. It takes the form of a prayer because that reflects
my spirituality. A Wiccan author might do something similar
by casting a quick, simple spell. I direct the prayer to Woden
and finish this with an Old English expression because I am a
Saxon Pagan. A Gallic Pagan writer would more likely direct
his or her own prayer to Ogmios, a Celtic god of eloquence
who was worshiped throughout Gaul. And, of course, the purpose of the ritual itself is directly related to my profession as
a writer. Saxon Pagans who work as salespeople or nurses or
research scientists would devise entirely different rituals more
appropriate for their respective lifestyles.

Your unique rites to sacralize daily activities need not be
limited to your work. In the following chapters we will explore
a variety of ways to reconnect with the earth, and all of them

involve imbuing otherwise mundane activities with a sacred mindfulness. Whatever hobbies you might have—jogging, playing a musical instrument, art, keeping tropical fish—can be sacralized.

Tropical fish, you say? Well, why not? Whenever we interact with other creatures, we connect more with the earth, so sacralize your tropical fish hobby! For a Hellenic Pagan, an aquarium can be a place to commune and speak with the naiads (water nymphs). A Roman Pagan might offer a prayer to Volturnus, god of the waters, as he feeds his fish. A Welsh Pagan with a saltwater aquarium could do the same, praying instead to Dylan Eil Ton. Exactly what you do and which spirits you connect with will, of course, depend on your spiritual focus. You could go so far as to decorate your aquarium with a theme that reflects your spiritual path.

Or do you play a musical instrument? Before you play, ask Apollo or Hathor or the Muses for inspiration. Give an offering as you ask for inspiration. Integrate your passion for music with your spiritual life. Let your private performance *be* your offering when you come before your gods. The effort you invest in a musical performance is as worthy as the effort you would invest in any other offering.

Any worthwhile pursuit can be a sacred act.

Step 5: Observe Regular Húsles

As a Saxon Pagan, I observe a *húsel* once each month near the full of the moon. Húsel is an Old English word meaning "sacrifice" and is simply a more formal offering usually given to a specific spirit. Some Saxons call this a *faining*, which simply means a celebration. Whatever your path, there is probably a similar custom of formal worship, although it will have a different name and be observed in a different way. For the Wiccan, this time of worship is known as an *esbat*. For an Ásatrúar, it is a *blót*. On the day after the new moon, Hellenic Pagans give offerings to the Agathos Daemon, a spirit of good fortune.

It might be argued that these are all different kinds of ritual, and that is true, but they share several defining traits. They are more formal than a person's ordinary devotionals, they recur at specific times (often monthly), and they are often more likely to be observed with a group rather than by oneself.

Húsles, esbats, blóts, and other similarly recurring observances further ensure our connection with Spirit. (For the sake of convenience, I am going to use the term húsel here, because húsles are what I celebrate and it is the term I am most comfortable with. Feel free to substitute whatever recurring observance is appropriate for your own spiritual path.) To understand the importance of this deeper connection, think of how you interact with your friends and close relatives. On a daily basis you may connect with friends only by an occasional phone call or e-mail, but periodically you get together to share quality time. The húsel is the quality time you spend with your gods, your ancestors, and the indigenous spirits around you.

The húsel also takes much longer than a personal devotion. If celebrated with a group—and, at least for Saxon Pagans, this is the desired way to do it—the ritual itself is usually preceded or followed by feasting and fellowship. It is not unusual for a húsel to go on for hours, throughout the day and well into the evening. The recurring observances of some other Pagan paths may not be quite as extensive, but they almost always require more time than the average person spends at his or her altar on a typical day.

Observing regular húsles (or esbats or blóts or druid moons) is similar to the other steps you have taken to this point in that you are establishing a new habit. Setting aside time for our gods is not an instinctive behavior. Setting aside time is a pattern we must develop and nurture, whether it is the sacred time we are creating for our daily devotions or the time we devote to a húsel.

Step 6: Observe the Holy Tides

The majority of Pagans today celebrate or at least recognize eight seasonal holidays spaced equidistantly, or nearly so, throughout the year. This Neo-Pagan calendar originated with the religion of Wicca but is now accepted by Pagans from many different paths. In the next chapter we will examine the Neo-Pagan calendar and how you can adapt it to your own needs and environment.

Also called the Wheel of the Year, the high days or holy tides of the Neo-Pagan calendar are Imbolc (February 1st), the spring equinox (March 21st), Beltane (May 1st), the summer solstice (June 21st), Lughnasadh (August 1st), the autumn equinox (September 21st), Halloween (October 31st), and the winter solstice (December 21st). The names and dates often vary from one group of Pagans to another.

You may be among those Pagans who observe a different annual calendar. There is certainly nothing wrong with this. None of the Paleo-Pagan religions celebrated all eight of the holidays recognized by contemporary Pagans, and there is no reason why you need to do so. If you are comfortable with the Neo-Pagan Wheel of the Year, then stick with that, but there is nothing inherently wrong with following a different sacred calendar.

The important thing is not what calendar you follow, but that you consistently observe the holy tides—the holidays—of that calendar. By doing so you touch the earth, attuning yourself to the seasonal changes occurring around you.

In the next chapter we will look at how you can adapt a sacred calendar to your own environment, and how you can make the holy tides more meaningful and fulfilling.

Step 7: Find Your Folk

Every step you have taken so far has been or could be a solitary action. You have had complete control over each one. You decided where and when you would make the effort to connect with Spirit. You alone designed your sacred space and designated a sacred time to consistently maintain your connection with your gods and ancestors. You have sacralized your daily actions and observed consistent húsles (or esbats or druid moons) and holy tides. You may have done some of this with other people, but it was entirely your choice to take action. For this seventh step, however, there is an element of chance. Depending on your circumstances, months or even a few years might pass before you cross paths with people whom you would want to weave your destiny with.

There are Pagans who remain "solitary" throughout their lives, eschewing any outward, communal spiritual expression. Humans, however, are social, tribal creatures, and the overwhelming majority of us are happier when we can share our life experiences with others. It is a rare person who enjoys spending New Year's Eve alone or looks forward to eating a Cornish game hen by himself on Thanksgiving Day. Our celebrations, whether secular or spiritual, are more fulfilling when we are joined with others of like mind.

For Saxon Pagans, this social collective is often called an *inhíred*, which is an Old English word meaning "household." Followers of Ásatrú have similar tribal units known as *kindreds*. A Hellenic Pagan is more likely to call his or her group a *demos*. Just as with the húsel or esbat, whether you call it an inhíred or a demos is not important here. These Pagan tribes vary a lot superficially, but they all (ideally) provide social support for their individual members.

The tribe may even be a nuclear family: Mom, Dad, and the kids. More often, however, it will be an extended "family of choice," composed of people who are not all genetically related. One such group may consist of two nuclear families and several other adult members, while another group may consist of five unrelated people. What all of the members do share is a common worldview.

I cannot overemphasize the value of the tribe. Pagan holy tides are no different than any other holidays; they can be lonely times if we have nobody to share them with. When I am unsure of a course of action, I can rely on my fellow gesithas (the oathed members of my inhíred) to give honest but gentle advice. When one of us needs help, the rest of us are there for him or her. We celebrate a húsel together every month and gather for holiday celebrations like any other family.

Because the tribe can become so very important in your life, it is equally important that you find the right people to enter into such a relationship with. This is where the element of chance comes in. As with finding a life partner, finding your folk is not a simple matter of looking through the Yellow Pages.

It can be tempting to join the first group you encounter, especially if you have been looking for other like-minded people for a long time. Before agreeing to join with any Pagan group, you should ask yourself the following questions:

- Does the group share your personal worldview? If not, how far are you willing to compromise your spiritual identity? What connects you to this tribe?
- What are the tribe's expectations of its members? Are these expectations clearly defined?
- What is required to leave the tribe if you later choose to do so? If a membership oath is involved, is there a provision in the oath allowing you to leave the group honorably? (The wording of some oaths do not require this, but be sure that you understand exactly what you are promising.)
- Does the group or its leaders take an undue interest in recruiting new members? This should raise a red flag. Pagan groups do not normally recruit.
- Do the other members of the group share a lifestyle compatible with your own? If you are single and in your twenties, you may not fit well with a group of retired couples. Or maybe you would, but it is a factor to consider.

If you are not completely satisfied with the answers to any of these questions, it is better to wait until you have found a group that you are sure of. An inhíred or demos or coven is not, or should not be, merely a social club. Membership in the group is an emotional contract that you should not enter into lightly.

This is why there is an element of chance. With the first six steps that I have outlined, you have complete control. You decide to take those actions. You do not have complete control over this seventh step. So while I have said "find your folk," it may be more accurate to describe this as leaving yourself open to finding your folk. To some extent, the process is in the hands of the gods.

I should add here that these tribes can and do sometimes overlap. It is never a good idea to "collect" covens or kindreds, but a Pagan may belong to more than one tribe when the groups have different objectives and nonconflicting schedules. The oathed members of my inhíred are all Saxon Pagans. We honor the same gods and share similar values. However, I also belong to an Ár nDraíocht Féin grove. The grove's purpose is to foster spiritual community in our immediate area. Not everyone in my inhíred belongs to the grove. Conversely, members of my grove do not have to be Saxon Pagans. These are two separate tribes, with different parameters and objectives. However, it is not a good idea to belong to two groups with similar objectives—two Wiccan covens, for example—because there will almost inevitably be competition for your time and energy. This is another reason you should only become a member of a group that you are completely comfortable with. Once you have your tribe, you cannot reasonably participate in other groups of the same type.

Now you have read about all seven steps. How many of these have you taken? If the answer is "none," go back now and start with step 1. Rather than simply reading about Paganism, take that first step and begin to walk the walk.

In the following chapters we will explore various activities that can take your personal Pagan practice to even deeper levels, but this "seven-step program" will lead you to a new way of living almost immediately. The steps are very simple. Eventually you will probably elaborate on some of them—establishing a secondary altar, or sacralizing more of your daily schedule—but the initial steps are easy actions anyone can take.

The only thing you might find difficult, especially if you are new to Paganism, is observing the holy tides. Depending on your lifestyle and environment, some of the high days may not seem relevant to you. In the next chapter we will look at the sacral calendar and how you can adapt it to your own life.

CHAPTER TWO

THE SACRAL CALENDAR

A calendar is a system for reckoning time by defining the beginning and divisions of a year. The secular calendar we all share today divides the year into twelve months of twenty-eight to thirty-one days, and begins the year on the first day of January. Most calendars define a year as the length of time it takes for our planet to orbit the sun, but there are exceptions. The Islamic sacral calendar is purely lunar, so each Islamic New Year begins eleven to twelve days earlier than the year before. Most calendars divide the year into twelve or thirteen months, based on the moon's orbit around our planet.

These divisions define the passage of time in a way that gives it meaning. For those of us who live in the temperate Northern Hemisphere, January evokes memories of ice and snow, June of warm afternoons, and October of crisp autumn leaves. A sacral calendar should create an even deeper meaning reflecting our spirituality. It *should* do this, but very often the calendar fails in its purpose because of the tendency many of us have to accept and follow a generic sacral calendar regardless of how appropriate it may or may not be for ourselves.

As a sacral calendar, the Neo-Pagan Wheel of the Year is a nice construct that all contemporary Pagan people can acknowledge when we get together with others of disparate paths. I like to think of it as the Esperanto of Pagan calendars; it does not belong to any one culture, but it is nevertheless a simple yet expressive way for all Pagans to measure the passage of the seasons. For the eclectic Pagan, the Neo-Pagan Wheel of the Year is as good a choice as any other for a primary sacral calendar.

The Neo-Pagan calendar observes eight holy days. This calendar can just as accurately be called the Wiccan sacral calendar, because it originated with the Wiccan religion in the early to middle twentieth century. The calendar combines Celtic fire festivals like Samhain and Beltane with Anglo-Saxon solstice celebrations. This amalgamation was hammered into a calendar of eight "sabbats" spaced five to seven weeks apart. Today it is used as a sacral calendar not only by Wiccans but also by many contemporary Pagan groups such as the Church of All Worlds and Ár nDraíocht Féin.

However useful the Neo-Pagan calendar may be, your own personal sacral calendar will be more meaningful to you if it reflects your spiritual path. Unless you follow the Wiccan religion, assuming you follow a specific path, your spiritual culture will have a calendar with unique emphases.

As a Saxon Pagan, I observe a Saxon calendar. The early, pre-Christian Saxons had a lunar-based calendar, but, unlike with the Islamic calendar, the solar year was also taken into consideration. Most years have twelve months, or "moons," but every few years there will be a *thrilithe*, which has thirteen months. The thrilithe adjusts the lunar calendar so the month of Solmonath always occurs around February, Hrethmonath always occurs around March, and so on. For the early Saxons, a new "monath" began at the full of the moon. In southern Europe—in Rome and Greece—a month began at the new moon, but in the northern European cultures it seems the months were reckoned by the full moons.

My inhíred gathers once a month to observe a húsel, giving offerings to our gods, but these "months" are not Gregorian (secular) months. They are true *monthas*, or moons. Because of this, we are keenly aware of the moon's cycles. Remember that Hal Sidu is all about integrating your body, mind, and spirit. By following a lunar-based calendar, my híredmenn and I attune ourselves to the rhythm of the natural world and, of equal importance, with the ways of our Saxon predecessors.

The lunar months help us connect with the worldview of the early Saxons and thus express our spirituality more fully. Solmonath, which falls in January and February, literally means "mud-month" in Old English. The historian Bede recorded that the Saxons gave offerings of cakes during this month. By cake he meant a baked product that was probably more like our modern bread. When the Solmonath moon grows full, I leave a loaf or cake on tilled soil as an offering.

The two months following, Hrethmonath and Eostremonath, are named for the earth goddess Herthe and the vernal goddess Eostre. After this comes Thrimilci, "three-milkings," so named because the cattle could be milked three times a day.

The next two months are Ærra Litha and Æfterra Litha. The Old English word *lith* means a point or moment, and in this context it is a reference to the summer solstice, that point in time when the days cease to increase in length and begin to decrease. The names of these two months, Ærra Litha and Æfterra Litha, mean "Before the Solstice" and "After the Solstice." Incidentally, during a thrilithe, the thirteenth month is inserted between these two and is known simply as Litha.

Next comes Weodmonath, or "weed-month," and, if you have ever had any connection with the earth, you understand why it has this name. Weodmonath occurs around August, when weeds grow like…well, like weeds…in the summer's heat in the temperate Northern Hemisphere. Then comes Haligmonath, the "holy-month," when offerings are given in thanks for a successful harvest.

It is almost always sometime in October when the Winterfylleth moon grows full. This month, as its name suggests, signals the beginning of winter. At this time, Saxon Pagans celebrate Winter Finding. It is not the end of the year, but it is an important transitional month that leads into Blodmonath, or the "blood-month." Winter began for the early Saxons with a final harvest—the harvest of meat. Only the best livestock would be wintered over, and the excess was butchered, smoked, and salted.

The final two months are Ærra Geola and Æfterra Geola, meaning "Before Yule" and "After Yule." The meaning of *Yule* is uncertain, but it may mean "wheel." Both of these months comprise the Yule season. Ærra Geola marks the end of the old year, while Æfterra Geola is the beginning of the new.

Observing the lunar months is an important aspect of my personal spiritual practice, but the Saxon calendar also acknowledges holy tides—holidays—at various times of the year. These holy tides correspond more closely to the Neo-Pagan calendar than those of some other Pagan paths. This is because Gerald Gardner, the founder of Wicca, was an Englishman. While the Neo-Pagan calendar is often thought to be Celtic in origin, the fact is that it is simply English, blending both Celtic and Anglo-Saxon holy days. Beltane and Samhain are Celtic fire festivals welcoming in the summer and winter. Yule and Midsummer are Anglo-Saxon festivals marking the summer and winter solstices. Lughnasadh is a summer festival commemorating the Celtic god Lugh and his foster mother; the Anglo-Saxons celebrated a grain festival called *Hláfmæsse* at the same time of year. The feast of the Anglo-Saxon goddess Eostre was celebrated at the full moon following the spring equinox, but has become equated with the equinox in the Neo-Pagan calendar. Of course the pre-Christian Saxons and Celts lived together on an island roughly the size of Missouri, so cultural exchange was inevitable, and Pagans today who follow a Welsh or Scottish path will also find that their personal spirituality blends very well with the Neo-Pagan Wheel of the Year.

For the Welsh or Scottish Pagan, the holy tides of Beltane and Samhain are the most important celebrations. But it is Yule that takes precedence on the Saxon calendar. It includes both months of Ærra Geola and Æfterra Geola, and celebrations might take place at any time during these two months. The most important part of Yule is Mothers' Night, the night of the winter solstice, when praise and offerings are given to our female ancestors, the mothers of our mothers. Today's Saxon Pagans usually focus their celebrations on Mothers' Night and the twelve nights that follow, ending on or just after New Year's. In my home we light one candle on Mothers' Night, two candles the following night, three the night after that, and so on until twelve candles are burning brightly on the twelfth night of our celebrating. We will discuss Yuletide activities in more depth in the final chapter of this book.

By observing the lunar cycles and traditional Saxon holy days, I honor not only my gods but also the ways of my ancestors. By this I mean my spiritual ancestors. I do happen to have a good measure of English blood, with family names like Potter, Oak, and Taunton in my pedigree, but the pre-Christian Anglo-Saxons are the spiritual ancestors of *any* Saxon Pagan, regardless of his or her biological ancestry. It is the worldview of the early Anglo-Saxons and their reverence for the earth that has inspired today's Saxon Pagans and shaped us, in part, to be who we are.

In addition to the months and seasons, a Saxon can incorporate the days of the week into his or her sacral calendar. It can be argued that the seven-day week originated with the Romans, but this construct was adopted very early in Saxon society. The English names for the days of the week are a veritable parade of Saxon divinity: Sunne, Mona, Tiw, Woden, Thunor, and Frige. The only exception is Saturday, which retained in its name the reference to the Roman god Saturnus. We may never know the reason for this, but, since Saturnus was a god of sowing, I think of Saturday as a day sacred to the god Ing and the goddess Fréo, divine siblings closely associated with the wealth of the earth.

My Saxon sacral calendar is a part of my personal practice of Hal Sidu. It is a holistic calendar. Rather than accept a
generic, one-size-fits-all Wheel of the Year, it is a reflection of
my spirituality. If you are a Pagan who follows a different path,
you will want to tweak the calendar in a different way, but the
principle remains the same. *Your* Wheel of the Year should be
relevant to *your* spirituality.

The names of the Saxon months (such as three-milkings
and weed-month) show that the calendar is predominantly
agrarian. This is not unusual for traditional Pagan methods
of reckoning the passage of time. To learn something about
the Irish sacral calendar, I spoke with my friend Diane Dahm,
an Irish Pagan who asserts that her own sacral calendar has
a similar focus. "Keep in mind that the significance of these
holidays had much to do with survival and were not always
the celebrations we view them as today," she says. "When
people were dependent on the earth and on the animals
for their source of food, acknowledging the turning of the
wheel was very much linked to where their food supply was
going to be coming from."

Diane is aware that the traditional Irish sacral calendar is
not the same as the Neo-Pagan calendar. "Instead of the eight
Neo-Pagan holidays, the Irish people observe four major festivals throughout the year: Samhain, Imbolc, Beltane, and
Lughnasadh." As an active member of her local Pagan community, Diane participates in group solstice and equinox rites,
but her personal sacral calendar emphasizes the four holy tides
that reflect her spirituality.

She also knows that the popular, modern interpretations
of those four holidays are not necessarily traditional Irish

Pagan interpretations. Diane believes that today's Pagans sometimes miss the deeper significance of holy tides like Beltane and Imbolc. In her own words, "Beltane is seen by Pagans today as being a fertility rite, but imagine the significance of the fertile earth…when your survival depends upon it. [Beltane] isn't as much about sex as it is about the potential for life to grow once again." She adds that "animals were often led between two fires to bestow blessings upon them for the upcoming year," a custom rarely seen in contemporary Beltane rites. Of Imbolc, the winter festival, Diane says, "Imbolc is commonly associated with the lactating of the ewes. In Irish society, wool was an important part of the economy, so it seems natural that this would be observed in some way. On the Christian calendar, February 1st is the Feast of St. Brigid. Presently, many Pagans honor the goddess Brigid in some way on this holiday, although it is unclear whether this is an ancient Pagan practice."

The Irish sacral calendar and the Saxon calendar are similar in their agricultural focus, but Diane makes it clear that there are also distinct differences between the two. The Winterfylleth moon in October marks the beginning of winter for Saxon Pagans, but for the Irish Pagan this time of year, known as Samhain, means much more. "The Irish marked the start of the New Year with Samhain, observed on the eve of November 1st and throughout the following day," says Diane. "Samhain is neither a day of this year or next. It stands on its own as a time between times. The Irish thought it to be neither summer nor winter, and the boundaries between the spirit world of the sidhe and the world of men were easily crossed."

Diane and I have different sacral calendars because we follow different spiritual paths. We can both relate to the Neo-Pagan calendar, but we each do so in a slightly different way. Spiritual cultures that evolved farther away from England will have sacral calendars that vary more from the Neo-Pagan calendar.

Hellenismos, also known as Hellenism or Hellenic religion, is Greek Paganism. Worship is directed to the Greek gods: Zeus, Hera, Apollo, Aphrodite, and so on. With a spiritual culture originating in southern Europe, Hellenic Pagans have a sacral calendar that bears little resemblance to the Neo-Pagan calendar. Irisa MacKenzie, a Hellenic Pagan living in Ohio, says, "The Hellenic calendar was based on a lunar cycle. As such, this affected their worship." Here we see a similarity between the Hellenes and the Saxons. Like the Saxons, the Hellenic people inserted a thirteenth month into their calendar every few years so the lunar months would fall into place with the solar year. This thirteenth month usually (but not always) followed their month of Poseideion, which falls in December and January. Irisa echoes Diane Dahm's comment about the Irish sacral calendar, saying, "The Hellenic calendar does not mirror the traditional Neo-Pagan Wheel of the Year. Aside from (some Hellenic festivals) being celebrated during a similar time frame, there is little in common with the modern Wheel of the Year."

One significant difference between the Hellenic sacral calendar and that of the Saxons, as Irisa has pointed out to me, is that the Hellenic month is reckoned from the dark of the moon, which is known as the Hekate Dephinion. This time was sacred to the goddess Hecate. The following day, when the moon can first be seen as a slender crescent in the evening sky, is known as the Noumenia, when offerings are given to all of the Hellenic gods, but in particular to Selene, Apollo, Hera, Hermes, and the household's ancestors.

The day following this is the day sacred to the Agathos Daemon. Irisa describes this as "the spirit that resides in your home, most commonly viewed as a snake, the ancient symbol of healing. Typically, a libation is given to the Agathos Daemon honoring its place in the home." The name Agathos Daemon simply means "noble spirit."

The third day after the new moon is sacred to the goddess Athena, and the day after that to both Aphrodite and Hermes. Days six and seven are sacred to Artemis and Apollo, respectively. The eighth day after the new moon is sacred to the god Poseidon.

At the full moon, the goddess Selene is again honored.

Each of the Hellenic months is sacred to an Olympian god or goddess. At the beginning of the month, at the Noumenia, Irisa gives a libation to that month's honored deity. In Athens, the year began when the new moon was first seen after the summer solstice. This signaled the month of Hekatombaion, which is sacred to Athena. During this month, the people of Athens celebrated the Panathenaia, a festival honoring the goddess of their city that usually came near the end of July. Irisa describes the Panathenaia as "a time of libations, games, and feasting."

The next month is Metageitnion, the month sacred to the god Hermes. A minor festival known as the Hera Thelchinia falls on the twentieth day of the month. This is celebrated by

Hellenic Pagans today with incense, hymns, and libations to the goddess Hera.

Following this is Boedromion, a month sacred to both Demeter and Persephone. Five days after the new moon during this month is the Genesia, a day to honor the dead, especially those who died in battle.

The month of Pyanopsion brings a festival called the Thesmophoria, which begins on the eleventh day of the month. This is usually celebrated by Hellenic women as a three-day festival, although Irisa tells me that some sources describe it as originally being a five-day festival. Whether three days or five, it is a women's festival. The rites involve fasting (except for pomegranate seeds), a torch ceremony, and a feast at the end.

Maimakterion is a month where nothing much seems to take place in the way of festivities. Historically, there was a feast during the latter part of the month called the Pompaia, dedicated to Zeus, but little is known about it, and it is not widely observed by contemporary Hellenes.

The sixth month is Poseideion, which, despite its name, is sacred to Dionysus. You would think that a month called Poseideion would be sacred to Poseidon, but those crazy Greeks sometimes had inscrutable ideas. On the twenty-sixth day of the month is a festival called the Haloa, sacred to both Demeter and Dionysus, and celebrated with much revelry. The people in Athens had a minor celebration at this time called the "Rural Dionysus," to distinguish it from the Greater Dionysus festival that takes place in the month of Elaphebolion. During the Rural Dionysus, a statue of the god was symbolically carried into the city. This event was followed by feasting and singing.

The month of Gamelion falls in January and February and is sacred to the goddess Hera. On the twenty-sixth day of the month, a festival called the Gamelia celebrates the marriage of Hera and Zeus, as well as the coming of spring and new beginnings.

This is followed by Anthesterion, a month sacred to Aphrodite. It is notable for its Anthesteria, or "Festival of Flowers," a three-day celebration that does not seem to actually have much to do with flowers. For Hellenes living in a northern temperate climate, this is probably a good thing, because the Anthesteria usually comes at some time around the end of February, when there is not very much in bloom. The festival begins on the eleventh day of the month with Pithiogia, or "opening of jars." New bottles of wine are opened and libations poured to Dionysus. The next day is Khoes, the "day of cups," when a lot of that wine is consumed in drinking contests. Irisa describes the festivities as having "an erotic atmosphere." The three-day Anthesteria ends with Khytrai, the "day of pots," when pots of food are set out as offerings for the dead.

After Anthesterion comes the month of Elaphebolion, which is sacred to Hephaestos. This is the month of the Greater Dionysus festival. The Greater Dionysus is celebrated with theatrical, poetic, and artistic competitions. Irisa says it is also "a time for the folk to let their inhibitions down." She mentions that images of phalluses were traditionally carried about in processions, so the festival probably had more of the erotic atmosphere that people had a taste of in the month of Anthesterion during the Khoes celebration.

(Anthesterion and Elaphebolion seem to be good months to be a Hellenic Pagan.)

The month of Mounykhion is sacred to the goddess Artemis, and on either the sixth day or the sixteenth comes the Mounykhia festival devoted to her. The discrepancy is because the Greeks did not have a standard, unified calendar. Either date can be celebrated as the Mounykhia by a Hellenic Pagan; however, you should probably pick one day or the other and stick to it.

It is fitting that Artemis's month is followed by Thargelion, which is sacred to her brother, Apollo. The sixth and seventh days of this month are a two-day festival called the Thargelia. Traditionally, in Athens, two people were selected to represent the entire city. These people were fed and then beaten to purify the city. So Thargelion may not be such a great month to be a Hellenic Pagan, at least not if you are offered a part in the local Thargelia rites. I am kidding, of course; such a practice is unacceptable today, but some act of purification—perhaps ritual bathing or censing—is appropriate for a Thargelia rite in the early summer.

Finally, the Hellenic year comes to an end in the early summer with the month of Skirophorion.

A very devout Hellenic Pagan may go to the effort to work out a sacral lunar calendar from one year to the next, but an understanding of the Hellenic months will benefit anyone who follows this path. Even if you are not certain when the twentieth day of Metageitnion is, you can nevertheless hold a Thelchinia rite in August and offer incense and libations to the goddess Hera. Hellenic women can gather together in October to celebrate the Thesmophoria with a feast. While this may seem haphazard, we have seen that even the Paleo-Pagan Hellenes did not have one universal, standard calendar.

To enjoy a more holistic spirituality, Irisa incorporates the Hellenic calendar in her personal Pagan practice, just as Diane Dahm does with the Irish calendar and I do with a Saxon calendar. Thus, for each of us, the calendar becomes more relevant to our work as Pagan people. Your calendar should be equally relevant to *your own* spiritual path. What holidays were historically observed in your cultural tradition? How did those people define the passage of time?

Another important consideration when developing a personal sacral calendar is your local climate and ecosystem. The Neo-Pagan Wheel of the Year assumes that you live in the United Kingdom. The more your climate varies from that of Great Britain, the less relevant the traditional Wheel of the Year will be for you. The same sacral calendar cannot serve both the needs of Pagans living in Toronto and the needs of Pagans in New Orleans; even if those Pagans follow the same spiritual path, they live in completely different climates.

It will take at least one full year for you to develop a sacral calendar that is truly relevant for your local environment. To do this, you will need to put down the book, step away from the computer keyboard, turn off the television, go outdoors, and really look at the world around you. The rewards will be well worth the effort. During the coming year, try to discover the answers to the following questions:

- What trees grow in your immediate vicinity (meaning within ten miles of your home)? Are they deciduous or evergreen? If deciduous, at what time of the year do their leaves begin to change color? When do they drop their leaves? Be specific; know the exact month, and whether it is early or late in the month. We all know that they drop their leaves in the autumn.

- When does the first hard frost come? This is assuming you experience a hard frost at all, which you will not if you live in Miami or San Diego.

- When does the last frost come in the spring? Again, this is assuming you live in a temperate climate.

- When does the first snow fall? How late in the spring do you have snow? Do you have snow at all?

- What flowers bloom in your region? When do they first come into bloom? How long do they bloom?

- What birds live in your immediate vicinity? Are they migratory, or do they live there all year? If they migrate, when do they leave? When do they return?

- What mammals live in your immediate vicinity? Does their behavior change at different times of the year? How?

- If you live in an agricultural region, what crops are grown and harvested? When are these planted? When is the produce collected and distributed?

As you answer these questions, you will appreciate the importance of the environmental factor in developing a personal sacral calendar. You will nurture your own understanding of your environment, which you can then incorporate into your spiritual and magical work.

You may occasionally need to strike a compromise between your spiritual path and your environment, while at other times these issues may come together to form a unique synthesis in your sacral calendar. For example, if you are a Hellenic Pagan living in Minneapolis, it can be difficult to reconcile the festival of Haloa with the frigid Minnesota winters. For the Greeks, Haloa was a harvest festival where recently gathered fruits were gratefully offered to Demeter and Dionysus, but Haloa usually falls in the Gregorian month of December, after the harvest season has come and gone in the northern United States. Of course we can give thanks for the gods' blessings at any time of year, and fresh fruit is available at our supermarkets regardless of the season. The northern Hellenic Pagan could celebrate Haloa by offering fruits to Demeter and Dionysus, but think about how this Greek festival could be incorporated more fully into a personal sacral calendar. Most of the Pagans I know enjoy the secular trappings of Christmas. In a Hellenic household, the solstice tree could be decorated with small, artificial fruits as a reminder of Demeter's bounty. An "angel" tree topper could be modified as an image of Dionysus by anyone with even moderate artistic skills. Ornaments shaped like pigs or bulls are appropriate, if they can be found, as these animals are sacred to Demeter and Dionysus, respectively. Ivy is also sacred to Dionysus, so garlands of artificial ivy could be used to decorate the tree and elsewhere in the home.

The solstice almost always comes after Haloa, but the two days are not far apart, so it would be very easy to incorporate the Hellenic festival into one's seasonal "Christmas" activities.

Of necessity, Pagans living south of the equator have adapted a sacral calendar to their own environment. The Pagans of Australia, South Africa, and Argentina have reversed the Neo-Pagan holidays. They celebrate Midsummer in December because, for them, June is mid-winter rather than mid-summer. Their spring equinox comes in September, and the autumn equinox in March. On the surface this seems simple and straightforward, but reversing the calendar changes the tone of the Neo-Pagan holidays. For Pagans south of the equator, it is at the summer solstice, not the winter, when most of their neighbors are celebrating the birth of Christ!

A Pagan living in the Southern Hemisphere also needs to determine whether or not each Pagan holiday is truly seasonal. Many traditional Pagan holidays—perhaps the majority—are seasonal because the production and acquisition of food was so very important in pre-industrial cultures. In northern Europe, especially, most holidays were related in some way to planting crops, harvesting, the birth of livestock, or some other aspect of agriculture. But this is not a universal quality. Looking again at the Hellenic calendar, there is no discernible reason why it would make any difference to observe the Panathenaia Festival in the winter instead of the summer. Nevertheless, some Pagans in the Southern Hemisphere may choose to reverse this holiday, too, holding it after their December summer solstice. There is no "correct" answer unless a holiday is obviously and undeniably seasonal. Two hundred years from now, Pagans may look back to see how and when people in the twenty-first century observed these holidays, but today, if you live in anywhere in the Southern Hemisphere, you must rely on your own intuition and good judgment for guidance.

But what about Pagans who live *on* the equator? While writing this chapter I began to wonder about this, so I asked my friend Mario Munive Avendaño. Mario lives in Bogotá, Colombia, where "winter" and "summer" are almost abstract concepts. "Here in Colombia we don't speak about winter solstice or summer solstice," he told me. "Here we have two seasons only: the dry season and the rain season....The rain season is April to October, and it rains so much. The rivers grow and the temperature falls a little, and the air is wet the majority of the time." This climate can be easily incorporated into the personal sacral calendars of Colombian Pagans by celebrating the advent of the rainy season each year at the March equinox. Whether March 21st is considered the "spring" equinox or the "autumn" equinox is largely irrelevant; it is the "rain" equinox!

Mario, who is a Wiccan, tells me that "many Wiccans in Colombia do their practice as if living in the North Hemisphere." This seems to be the default, since there is no real reason for Colombians to reverse the Neo-Pagan holidays. The same Northern Hemisphere default favored by Colombian Wiccans would work equally well for Roman, Slavic, Hellenic, or Saxon Pagans in Colombia, but a truly relevant sacral calendar should also observe the dry and rainy seasons at the appropriate times, since these are such prevalent forces in that equatorial climate.

What Colombia lacks in seasonal change it makes up for with its numerous national holidays. The month of February is especially notable for its celebrations, with annual carnivals held in cities like Barranquilla, Santa Marta, and Riohacha. Mario says there are festivals held in Colombia throughout the year, including "some so bizarre, like a donkey festival in some little town in Colombia, I cannot remember (where) now." Which leads us to another consideration when creating a personal sacral calendar. Whether you live near the equator, like Mario, or near the polar ice cap, regional celebrations often can and should be acknowledged as spokes in your own Wheel of the Year.

At first it may seem that there is a vast difference between a holy day like Beltane and a national secular holiday like Veterans Day, but that difference diminishes for those who seek to follow Hal Sidu. Why should one moment in your life be any less sacred than another? For some people a secular holiday like Veterans Day may mean nothing more than the banks closing. But any secular holiday can reflect your spirituality, and in fact many American Ásatrúar observe Veterans Day as a holy day they call Einherjar, or the Feast of the Einherjar. By doing so they have incorporated Veterans Day into their sacral calendars. The Einherjar are the spirits of warriors who have fallen in battle, those who have been taken up to Valhalla. The Einherjar are typically reverenced with a *blót*, a ritual in which mead (honey wine) is offered to the honored spirits.

Any secular holiday can be sacralized in this way and given a special place in your personal calendar. Valentine's Day? A Hellenic Pagan could give libations to Aphrodite (the Hellenic goddess of love), while a Norse Pagan could offer mead to the goddess Freya. Or if Arbor Day is meaningful to you, incorporate it into your sacral calendar as a day to honor dryads, wood elves, or however else you perceive the spirits of the trees. Thanksgiving Day is self-explanatory. For American Pagans, Thanksgiving is essentially a fourth harvest festival, following in the wake of Lammas, the autumn equinox, and All Hallows Eve.

Since 1970, Earth Day has been observed in the United States every year on April 22nd to inspire a greater awareness of the environment. I have sacralized the observance with the following ritual to the earth goddess Herthe. The wording is based on a prayer from an eleventh-century book of Anglo-Saxon herbal charms (although it is probably much older), while the offerings are inspired by another eleventh-century charm known as the Æcerbot, or "Field Remedy." As a celebration of the earth, the ritual is intended to be held outside. If held indoors because of inclement weather or for any other reason, there must be a bowl to receive the offerings. These offerings should later be poured out onto the earth. In an outdoor ritual, the offerings are individually poured onto the earth as libations.

Up to seven *gebedmenn* (prayer-leaders) can have active roles in the ritual. If there are fewer than seven participants, individual gebedmenn may take more than one part. For that matter, one person can perform this devotional ritual alone. You will need:

- A fire or (if indoors) a charcoal and a burner to hold it.
- A pinch of fennel seeds.
- A small quantity of natural pressed vegetable oil.
- A small quantity of honey.
- A small quantity of whole milk.

The *finol gebedmann* (fennel prayer-leader) sprinkles a pinch of fennel seeds into the fire (or onto the burning coal), saying:

> *Herthe, Divine Goddess, Mother Nature,*
> *who generates all things*
> *and brings forth anew the sun,*
> *which you have given to the nations.*

Now the *sceadu gebedmann* (shadow prayer-leader) says:

> *Guardian of sky and sea, of all gods and powers;*
> *through your power all nature falls silent,*
> *and then sinks into sleep.*
> *And again you bring back the light, and chase away the night,*
> *and you cover us yet most securely with your shadows.*

The *storm gebedmann* (storm prayer-leader) comes forward and says:

> *You contain chaos infinite, yes, and wind and showers and storms.*
> *You send them out when you will and cause the sea to roar;*
> *you chase away the sun and arouse the storm.*

Following this, the *lif gebedmann* (life prayer-leader) says:

> *Again, when you will, you send forth the joyous day*
> *and give the nourishment of life with your eternal surety.*
> *And when the soul departs, to you we return.*

The *ele gebedmann* (oil prayer-leader) pours a libation of oil while saying:

> *You are duly called the Great Mother of the Gods;*
> *you conquer by your divine name.*
> *You are the source of strength of nations and of gods.*

The *hunig gebedmann* (honey prayer-leader) steps forward and pours a libation of honey, saying:

> *Without you, nothing can be brought to perfection or be born;*
> *You are great, Queen of the Gods.*

The *meolc gebedmann* (milk prayer-leader) pours a libation of whole milk and says:

Goddess, I adore you as divine;
I call upon your name
and give thanks to you, with due faith.

At this time the finol gebedmann may invite any who wish to do so to speak their own personal words of praise, or to make oaths to honor or protect the earth in some way. This is a good time to reaffirm a commitment to Hal Sidu by oathing to make some specific change in your lifestyle that will lead to a more holistic, positive existence.

Finally, the meolc gebedmann concludes the ritual by saying:

Hail to you, Herthe, Mother of Men and Gods.

To which all participants respond with a hearty "Wassail!"

I am a Saxon Pagan, so my Earth Day ritual includes Anglo-Saxon words and draws its inspiration from Old English writings, but anyone, whatever the source of his or her spiritual inspiration, can devise a similar rite to honor the earth every year on April 22nd.

Ideally, when you have met the challenge of devising a sacral calendar that is true to yourself, yours will not look exactly like everyone else's because our individual relationships with the world around us are shaped by a variety of factors. Your own sacral calendar should reflect your spiritual orientation, your physical environment, and the greater society in which you participate.

CHAPTER THREE

DAILY DEVOTIONS

Having a sacral calendar that reflects your environment and your spiritual focus is more meaningful than following a one-size-fits-all Wheel of the Year, but every day of the year—no matter how ordinary—can be invested with your spirituality. The holistic Pagan lives fully in the moment. Rather than waiting for a special calendar date to give praise to the gods and ancestors, each day is embraced as a new opportunity for spiritual expression.

Perhaps you already do this. How, if at all, have you expressed your spirituality today? Is it something you do every day, or was it a special or sporadic activity? Like your sacral calendar, you should approach each day in a way that is appropriate for your own spiritual focus and circumstances. Almost any moment of your life can have a deeper spiritual meaning, but those moments are unique to yourself. My day—influenced by my household and my means of support—is different from yours, just as your day is at least slightly different from that of most of your friends.

Whether we dash off to an office or to school, or enjoy a leisurely cup of coffee, or take the dog for a walk, the one thing most of us do each morning is rise to face a new day. Some people begin the day at an odd hour due to their occupational schedule, but the majority of us awaken in the morning. This event, so common and simple, is a great opportunity to affirm your spirituality. Some Pagans like to meditate in the morning, believing it better prepares them for the coming day. It need not be a lengthy meditation; ten minutes can be more than enough. If time is an issue, set your alarm fifteen minutes earlier, meditate for ten minutes, and then enjoy the extra five minutes of free time that you have given yourself.

A morning meditation is a great way to start the day—for some people. It does not work for everyone. You may be one of those people who are more likely to fall back asleep if you attempt to meditate that early in the day. If so, you can still sacralize the first moments of your day by connecting with Spirit with a short but sincere prayer.

I prefer to meditate later in the day, and instead greet the morning with a prayer. And I readily confess that I am not a "morning person," so it is best, for myself, if the words are prepared and ready to come from my lips. I am not very good at extemporaneous speaking when I first wake up. For this reason, I have a set prayer that I like to use in the morning. The prayer is to the goddess Sunne, sovereign spirit of the sun. As I address her, I usually mark the *sigel* rune in the air with my right hand. *Sigel* is the Anglo-Saxon rune that represents the sun.

The wording of the prayer is:

> *Hail to you, Sunne,*
> *Jewel of the Heavens,*
> *rightly are you called the Glory of Elves!*
> *Bright and fair,*
> *sailors' prayer,*
> *love's light woven through your hair.*
> *Giver of life, to you I pray,*
> *guide my steps throughout this day.*

The phrase "sailors' prayer" is inspired by the passage in the Anglo-Saxon Rune Poem that tells us "the sun, for sailors, is always hoped for when they depart over the fishes' bath" (*sigel sæmannum simble biþ on hihte, þonne híe hine fériaþ ofer fisces bæþ*). The expressions "Glory of Elves" and "Jewel of the Heavens" are old Germanic kennings for the sun.

A morning prayer to Sunne is appropriate for me as a Saxon Pagan, but the spirituality of a Hellenic (Greek) Pagan would be better reflected in a prayer to Helios, the Greek god of the sun, while a Kemetic (Egyptian) Pagan might direct his or her morning prayer to Ra. The Irish Pagan could pray to the goddess Éadaoin, and the Slavic Pagan to Dazhbog. These are all, of course, sun deities within their respective cultures. The form of the prayer and any gestures associated with it should also be culturally appropriate. Obviously a Kemetic Pagan is not going to mark the *sigel* rune while praying to Ra, since the Anglo-Saxon runes do not express Kemetic spirituality, but an *akhet* (the Egyptian symbol of the horizon where the sun rises) might be worn or held during the prayer.

While it is important that your morning prayer reflect your spiritual path, the deity you pray to does not necessarily need to be a solar or dawn deity. An Irish Pagan can offer a morning prayer to Éadaoin, but the prayer can as easily be directed to Brigid or the Dagda if that person has a strong connection to either of the deities. A Kemetic devotee of Isis might choose to direct a prayer to that goddess rather than to the sun god Ra. Here again, the important thing is that your prayer be true to your spiritual path. A solar deity from your cultural pantheon is an obvious choice to address in a morning prayer, but you are essentially giving thanks for a new day and all that it may bring, and that prayer can be directed to whatever god or goddess you feel a connection with.

SINGING IN THE SHOWER

Early morning is just one of many moments throughout the day that can be invested with meaning through prayer. If you find that praying just after you wake up is little more than an exercise in somnambulism, if your morning prayer sounds more like a discordant growl, it might be more effective for you to greet the day a little later.

You may find it easier and more meaningful to pray after you have had a cup of coffee and have rubbed the crusty bits of sleep from the corners of your eyes. If so, the morning shower is another good time to greet the day. While showering is a very physical, material act, on a spiritual level you

are also washing away the previous day and preparing yourself for what awaits in your immediate future. If you invest
the act of showering with your spirituality, it becomes a sort
of ritual in itself. You might use a prayer to your ancestors,
such as this:

> *Beloved ancestors,*
> *mothers who gave birth to my mothers,*
> *fathers who sired my fathers,*
> *wash away all that would impede me;*
> *diminish all that might pollute me.*
> *As the life-giving water flows over me,*
> *refresh and renew my spirit*
> *that I might through my actions give you due honor*
> *throughout the coming day.*

Or instead of a spoken prayer, you may be inspired to greet
the day with song. Do it! There is a reason why so many people like to sing as they shower. The design of a shower stall
often gives an acoustic effect that enhances the human voice.
There are many Pagan songs written by various artists today.
Your own song of praise could even be a secular song, like
"Oh, What a Beautiful Mornin'" from Rodgers and Hammer-
stein's *Oklahoma*. What matters is that the song expresses in
some way your joy and gratitude for the new day.

If you have any talent for it at all, try creating your own
words and melody for a song of praise. People do it all the
time. That is where new Pagan songs come from.

Transforming your daily shower into a ritual shower can
enhance your personal Pagan practice, but this same concept—

spiritual cleansing—can be extended to small rites of purification throughout the day. Wash your hands with a short prayer just before beginning any project. This is especially appropriate for Pagans who follow a Hellenic path. Ritual cleansing and changing into clean clothing is traditional for Hellenic rituals of any kind (Burkert, p. 55). Do you need to write a term paper? Wash your hands in a rite of purification before sitting down at the word processor. Preparing a meal? Wash off the miasma from your hands before you begin cutting and stirring.

BLESSING THE MEAL

Speaking of food, if you sit down to three square meals a day (and you should), you have three more opportunities to bring your spirituality into your daily life. Very often today, people approach their food almost as an afterthought, with no real awareness of what they are eating, how it was prepared, or where it came from. Later in this book we will look deeper into how you can reclaim your connection with the food that sustains you, but as a first step, why not acknowledge each meal with gratitude?

Whom will you express your gratitude to, and how? A simple verse will come more easily to the lips than a lengthy or extemporaneous prayer. You may prefer to say something thoughtful and very specific at a formal feast, such as the American celebration of Thanksgiving, but for daily practice the prayer should be undemanding. It can be as uncomplicated as the traditional Christian children's prayer, "God is great, God is good, and we thank him for our food."

Indeed, this prayer can be readily adapted to polytheistic worship by changing the wording from singular to plural:

"The gods are great, the gods are good, and we thank them for our food."

I use an adaptation of a prayer directed to the sun and the earth. My version addresses these as sentient beings: as Sunne, goddess of the sun, and Herthe, goddess of the earth.

Herthe, who gives to us this food,
Sunne, who makes it ripe and good,
Sunne above, Herthe below,
my loving thanks to you I show.

Of course when I am out at a restaurant, I do not stand up, wave my arms in the air, and loudly chant this prayer. In a public setting it is only civil to consider the sensibilities of others. I am not at all apologetic about my beliefs and practices (why should I be?), but those beliefs do not require me to act like an oaf. When a display of personal belief would be inconsiderate, every Pagan path has at least a few symbols that can be faintly traced on the table or over a dish before eating. Nobody will have due cause to take offense if your gesture is subtle. My preference is the symbol of Thunor's hammer, marked like this:

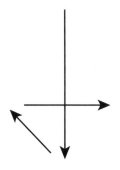

An Irish Pagan might trace the image of Brigid's cross. A Wiccan can trace the pentagram. As with everything else in your personal practice, the symbol should be a reflection of your own spirituality.

NOW I LAY ME DOWN TO SLEEP

Thus began the bedtime prayer I was taught to recite as a child. One line of the prayer mentioned that I might "die before I wake," which was a real possibility, but was nevertheless more than a little creepy for my preschool imagination. My parents were monotheists, as were their parents before them, so the prayer was directed to the biblical god. But just because a practice or tradition is Christian does not mean that it is not also Pagan.

As with the morning, the moments before you go to sleep are a good time to connect with and express your spirituality, but there are differences. In the morning, many of us are barely coherent, and the events of the day have yet to unfold. This is why a brief, prepared prayer often works better. The evening, though, is a time to reflect on what took place during the day. There will inevitably be specific things to give thanks for or to ask for guidance about. A memorized prayer might be suitable for a small child, but I have found that extemporaneous prayer is usually more appropriate in the evening. Mentally list everything good that happened to you over the course of the day.

If you cannot think of any good events, you probably need to dig deeper. It is highly unlikely that you are among the very few people who never have anything good happen to them. In my experience, the majority of those who feel that way do so because they take the good things in their lives for granted. Friends, family, your health, a source of income (even if this is modest), your home...these are all things to be thankful for. Today's Pagans *all* enjoy the blessings of the twenty-first century. Compared to most of our forebears, we live in luxury. We have light and, in the winter, heat at the touch of a switch. Food is readily available at the nearest supermarket regardless of any local drought or pestilence. These are wonderful blessings.

Happy people are those who notice that their cups are, indeed, half full. By reflecting on the good things that have happened throughout the day and then giving thanks for those blessings, you can join the ranks of the happy people.

Conversely, a prayer before going to bed is also a good time to acknowledge the half-empty portion of your cup. Look back on the day's challenges and on the mistakes you made, and ask for guidance. Whom exactly you ask for guidance from is your own choice. You might seek guidance from a god or goddess you have a personal connection with, but you may as easily ask your ancestors for advice. Put a sprig of rosemary under your pillow so you will remember any guidance they give you during the night when you awaken the following morning.

Since evening is a time for reflection, the bedtime prayer is also a good time in the day to offer prayers for those in need. These will usually, probably, be the people of your own tribe, whether you call this an inhíred or a coven or a kindred, but you may pray for anyone. Praying for others in the evening is another way of acknowledging your own blessings. It is more difficult to throw yourself a little pity party after you have offered a prayer for those confronting truly difficult challenges in their lives.

Children can be encouraged to think of others by having them send "moon wishes" in the evening before going to bed. After tucking your child into bed, ask whom he or she would like to send moon wishes to. You may need to prompt a very young child with several suggestions, but children very quickly catch on and enjoy this, naming siblings and other relatives, as well as school friends, whom they would like to bless. After the child has named all who would receive the moon blessings, the list of names can be followed with a prayer such as this:

> *Mona, who shines his light on me,*
> *On field and meadow, on hill and tree,*
> *Mona, who shines so bright above,*
> *bless the folk I know and love.*

I direct the moon wish prayer to Mona, the Saxon sovereign spirit of the moon, but it should not be difficult to alter the words to reflect your own spiritual path. All you need to do is change the name of the moon deity, and perhaps the gender if your path perceives the moon as a feminine spirit. An eclectic Pagan (someone who does not follow a specific path, but instead borrows from different cultures) could even direct this in a more generic way, saying, "Moon that shines its light on me," and so on.

DAILY OFFERINGS

So far we have looked at events that are part of your daily routine—awakening, bathing, meals, and bedtime—and these are only a few examples chosen from those activities we all share. I am sure that you can think of other daily events, unique to your own routine and lifestyle, that can be sacralized in ways similar to what has been described here. When we evoke the sacred in our normal activities, our lifestyles become holistic, and every day is transformed into a spiritual experience.

Beyond this, there are actions we can take to extend this experience even further into our lives. Wicca's fundamental tenets are embodied in the "Charge of the Goddess," an inspirational text composed by Doreen Valiente in which worshipers are called upon to meet "once in the month, and better it be when the moon is full." But this is *minimal* participation; nowhere in the short text does it say that Wiccans cannot or should not "dance, sing, feast, make music and love" at other times of the month. Whatever path you follow, you do not need to wait for a special phase of the moon, a sabbat, or a high day to honor the spirit realm. You are a spiritual being every day of the year!

One way to acknowledge the spirit realm on a daily basis is to make an offering to your house elves. Many Pagan cultures traditionally prayed and gave offerings to household spirits. The Saxons called these spirits *cofgodas*. The Romans called them *lares*. European folklore abounds with tales of small, fairy-like beings helping those mortals who show them honor and respect.

From those same tales we know that house elves usually appreciate offerings of milk or baked goods, or both. I pour a few ounces of milk into a cup in the evening and set this on the mantel over the fireplace. In the morning I pour whatever is left (house elves drink surprisingly little) down the drain. This is for an ordinary daily offering. If the gift to the house elves is part of a more extensive ritual, the milk is more likely to be left overnight on our household altar. Further, the offering is sometimes a food or drink other than milk, although milk is my usual choice for a daily offering.

If you intend to do this every day, keep it brief. The words you speak, if you say anything at all, can be as simple as, "Know that you are remembered by me and my household." That, in fact, is exactly what I say when I leave the offering for our house elves.

Some people have told me that their house elves like whiskey, ale, or another nondairy beverage; these are usually alcoholic. If you sense that your own house elves would like something besides milk or cake, try other things. Folklore warns us that the one thing you should never give them is clothing. The story "The Shoemaker and the Elves," retold with a variety of different titles over the years, can be traced back at least as far as the early 1800s when it was published by Jacob and Wilhelm Grimm, but elements of the tale are undoubtedly much older. In the Grimm version, a poor shoemaker and his wife find that their fortunes begin to change for the better when a pair of elves begin secretly assembling shoes in the shop late at night. To thank the elves, the shoemaker and his wife make two small shirts, two vests, two pairs of pants, and two small pairs of shoes, and then leave these out as gifts for their benefactors. The elves are delighted when they find the gifts, which they immediately put on. Then they dance out the door and are never seen again.

That's gratitude for you.

Why the elves left after being gifted with clothing is never explained, and any hypothesis can be no more than speculation. The point is that you should probably stick to foods and beverages when giving offerings to your own house elves.

Another approach to daily offerings, again depending on your spiritual focus, is offerings to your ancestors. Reverence for the ancestors is very important to many Pagans. Other Pagans have a difficult time with the idea of honoring their ancestors, usually because they have had a falling out with a parent or grandparent who has passed on, but this should be irrelevant because you have never actually met—in life—the majority of your personal ancestors. The dictionary defines *ancestor* as a forebear more remote than a grandparent; in other words, a *distant* forebear. So if you have a deceased grandfather who once treated you shamefully, keep in mind that he probably had to explain his behavior to his own great-grandmother when she met him Over There.

One nice thing about ancestral spirits is that they are predisposed to care about your well-being. You, after all, are their legacy to this world. Because of this predisposition, your offering can be almost anything you choose. As a daily offering, however, it needs to be relatively simple. The value is in the consistency of the offering rather than the worth of the gift on any particular day. A daily offering to one's ancestors can be a bit of incense or a small libation of wine or beer. As with an offering to your house elves, the words you speak when giving a daily offering to your ancestors should be brief.

Can you do both? Absolutely! I like to give an offering of incense to my ancestors in the mid-morning. There is no profound reason for this; it just fits my schedule well. Then in the evening my house elves receive their offering.

Or, if you feel that you have a close, personal relationship with a god or goddess, you might want to give a daily offering to that deity. The appropriate offering and how it is presented will vary from one deity to another and from one cultural practice to the next, but in general the rules for a daily offering hold true here as well. If you approach it as a lengthy, complex ritual, you simply will not do it every day. You might for a week or so, or perhaps for a month, but eventually life's incessant demands will interfere. You are much more likely to remain consistent with daily offerings if these take only a few moments of your time. If you have the luxury of being able to linger at your altar for an extra twenty minutes, that is great, but the additional time should not be scheduled into a daily ritual.

Consider, too, how many of these small rituals you can reasonably and consistently fit into your routine. If you pack in too much, these will cease to be special moments in your day and begin to seem more like arduous chores. I do not advise giving separate daily offerings to your house elves, your ancestors, and a deity. Pick one of these or, at the most, two. Do not take on more than you can handle in an enjoyable and meaningful way.

WHAT THIS DAY HOLDS FOR YOU

Another thing I like to do each morning is see what the day has in store for me. Whether or not you would benefit from this depends on how you feel about divination, and how proficient you are with it. I like to know what to expect of the coming day. At times I have changed my day's plans because of something I saw in my morning divination.

Because of my spiritual path, I use runes for divination, and specifically the runes of the Anglo-Saxon Futhorc. The study of runes is an extensive subject and far beyond the scope of this book. If you are interested in rune lore for either divination or magic, I recommend my book *Wyrdworking: The Path of a Saxon Sorcerer*.

If there is one thing you have learned from this chapter, it is that anything you hope to do on a daily basis must be simple and brief. This is equally true for a daily divination. When seeking an omen for the day, I do not lay out a complex Seven Worlds reading, and I certainly do not cast all twenty-nine runes on a cloth. These are techniques to use when looking for a detailed vision of how the future is unfolding. For my daily divination, I simply draw a single rune. It gives me a general idea of what the coming day will be like, and that is all I am looking for.

This morning, for example, I drew the rune *os*, which looks like this:

The Rune Poem describes the mystery of the rune: "The god is the creator of all language, wisdom's foundation and consolation of sages, and every man's joy and trust."

As you can see, this mystery is open to interpretation, which is what the study of rune lore is all about. (The word rune, *rún* in Old English, means mystery or counsel.) These symbols do not have easy, finite meanings. *Os* is a rune of communication. Exactly what that means depends on who is reading the runes, and whom he or she is reading them for. Whenever I draw *os* in a daily divination, I know it is a good day, for me, to sit down at the word processor and get some work done. That is what I did, and my day has been amazingly productive.

On days when I draw the rune *ethel*, for example, I am going to get more done if I focus on household chores rather than writing. I do not always have the luxury of adjusting my schedule in this way, but over the years I have learned to heed the advice of the runes when I can.

Runes, of course, are only one of many symbol sets used for divination, and these may not be appropriate if you follow a non-Germanic path. I have Celtic Pagan friends who prefer to use the symbols of the Beith-luis-nin, because these are directly related to their spirituality. A Slavic friend of mine uses a completely different set of symbols that reflect his own spiritual focus. The symbols are called *Znaki* (a word that simply means "symbols") and are derived from the designs used on Ukranian Easter eggs.

The Tarot originated in northern Italy in the fifteenth century, but many Pagans enjoy using these cards, and if you have studied the symbolism, then there is no reason you could not utilize a deck for your daily divination. You should still keep this very simple. Instead of placing cards in a Celtic Cross or some other Tarot spread, simply draw a single card to see what the day holds for you. You can use either the entire deck for this or just the twenty-two trump cards (sometimes called the cards of the "major arcana").

In the first chapter of this book, I advised against setting a goal of meditating every day simply because you are not going to do it. Yes, I realize that somebody out there is going to prove me wrong, meditating every single day for years on end, but the overwhelming majority of people who read this book will not be able to maintain such a goal no matter how sincere their intentions. Some interruption will intrude in your life, which can be frustrating and discouraging if you have a stated goal of meditating daily.

That said, I do think every Pagan can benefit from meditating as often as reasonably possible. If that is no more often than once a month or so, then once a month is what is "reasonably possible" for you. Set a schedule that you can keep up with.

To meditate, find a time when you can be undisturbed. Sit before your altar. If you find it helps, offer some incense to the spirits. Quiet your mind as well as you are able. Most people find that this is easiest if they focus on their breathing. Inhale to a slow count of four, hold the breath for an equal count, then exhale for an equal count. Continue with this until you are fully relaxed. Be aware of any sensations or impressions you may receive. Fifteen minutes is a good length of time to invest in this, but there is no set rule.

During your meditation you may receive mental impressions, or even have visions or hear voices. Simply accept what comes to you. After the meditation you may want to record these perceptions in a journal.

Or maybe nothing at all will happen. That is perfectly all right. Not everyone is exceptionally psychic, and even if you are, there will be times when the spirits just do not have much to say. In fact, if you are receiving profound psychic impressions during every meditation, you might want to step back and make sure your imagination is not working excessively. I am not unreasonably skeptical, but I also do not believe any of us are so important that spirits and deities are hovering nearby at every moment of the day, eagerly waiting to impart tidbits of wisdom. No matter who you are, there are times—more often than not—when your meditation will be nothing more than a brief respite from the pressures of the world.

Your daily devotions will be much more meaningful if your entire household is involved. Sadly, this is not always possible, and if others in your household follow a path different from your own, then that must be accepted. Ideally, though, the whole family will join together at a sacred hearth, sharing in their spirituality.

I have heard quite a few Pagan parents express concern about "forcing" their beliefs and practices on their children.

This sentiment inevitably originates with their own childhood experiences. I would never suggest forcing anyone to believe as I believe, or to practice as I practice, but there is a world of difference between sharing something and forcing it on another person.

I love broiled lobster tails with a side of melted butter. As crazy as it seems to me, I know there are people out there who do not care for lobster, and I would never try to force anyone to eat it. But given the opportunity, I will almost always try to share this epicurean delicacy with friends who are unfamiliar with it just because, in my opinion, it is incredibly delicious. Why would I do anything less with my spirituality? If your child gags on lobster, do not make him finish it but, for gods' sakes, at least let him try it!

It is true that children can suffer prejudice and bigotry if others learn of their family's Pagan beliefs, but this is usually not a problem if you avoid using, around younger children, the "hot" words likely to inflame the ignorant. It is very easy to be fully and devoutly Pagan without actually saying the word *Pagan* in front of your children. Definitely avoid the word *witch*, even if someone in your family practices magic. (It seems odd to me that I should even need to mention this, but you would be surprised at how many people openly announce that they are witches and then are amazed when small-minded coworkers or neighbors react with fear and anger.) Children have their own code of behavior, and nobody understands the importance of conformity more than a ten-year-old. By the time your child is old enough to coherently discuss your family's beliefs and practices, he or she will most likely comprehend the potential repercussions of doing so. If you are worried nevertheless, then talk with your child, but do not hide your beliefs and practices as if they are something to be ashamed of.

By the same token, I do not think it is a good idea to shield children from Christianity. Every Pagan child should be given a book of children's Bible stories. Whatever path you and your family may follow, the Bible has shaped our language and expressions, and your child should understand what is meant when somebody references Adam and Eve, the Flood and Noah's Ark, or the Tower of Babel.

You should never force your beliefs on your children (or anyone else, for that matter). Pagans are polytheists, believing in many different deities and, by extension, respecting many different spiritual paths. To demand that a child conform to one specific path is as un-Pagan as a demand can possibly be. But if you love your gods and find beauty in your spiritual path, then these are things you should share with your children to whatever extent they would like to join in with your own daily devotions.

CHAPTER FOUR

FAMILIAR SPIRITS

In the confessions obtained from medieval heresy trials, we can find repeated descriptions of the witch's familiar spirit. According to those confessions, the familiar could take the form of a human being, but more often it took the form of a beast, such as a dog, cat, bird, rat, or toad. Even today, a black cat is as much a part of the "witch" stereotype as a broomstick or a cauldron.

Margaret Murray (whose scholarship is admittedly questionable) divided familiars into two categories: Divining Familiars and Domestic Familiars. The former were simply animals that were observed, in the hope of perceiving omens. In *The God of the Witches*, Murray tells of a sixteenth-century woman named Agnes Sampson watching a large black dog to determine the eventual outcome of another woman's illness (p. 82). Whether the term *familiar* is descriptive for this category of beast at all is debatable, for there was nothing especially familiar about the animals. According to Murray, the Divining Familiar was not a specific animal that belonged to the witch; any animal of a given species could be used for divining the future. This was completely different from the Domestic Familiar, a (usually) smaller animal that was tamed and fed by the witch.

Although Margaret Murray's conclusions about a widespread, organized medieval witch cult have been largely discredited, there is no question that people were often accused during the witch trials of harboring animals matching Murray's description of Domestic Familiars. There are detailed reports of these familiar spirits. The animals were inevitably given names, sometimes quite ordinary and other times whimsical. Smaller animals like toads and mice were often housed in boxes, pots, and similar containers. Something devilish was obviously going on, because the witches actually fed their familiar spirits. Even more, the witch supposedly spoke to the animal as if it were a person.

As I write this, my dog Caesar lies curled up at my feet. He does not always stay there; Caesar is just as likely to retire to his crate when he does not want to be disturbed. Of course I feed him—twice each day, morning and night. So far as I know, he does not understand more than a couple dozen words, but I talk to him all the time.

Five hundred years ago, people were murdered for exhibiting such outlandish behavior as this.

There's no question about it: my dog Caesar is a familiar spirit! He fits all of the criteria. When we look at the descriptions of the witches' familiars, it can be seen that the dogs, cats, toads, and mice that were kept by the poor, unfortunate victims of the witch trials were what we now call companion animals. Not only is there no longer any superstitious stigma attached to animal companionship, the mental and physiological benefits of interactions with animals are widely accepted. Organizations like Therapy Dogs International and Canine Assisted Therapy bring the benefits of animal companionship to people who are unable to keep their own pets for various reasons. The magic of familiar spirits has indeed become widespread in our time!

A familiar spirit is a pet, but not every pet is a familiar spirit. The key word here, of course, is *familiar*. Some species—notably dogs and cats—lend themselves to this role better than others. We like to think that humankind domesticated these species, but an argument can be made that it is the human race that has been domesticated. True, we humans do not always play well with others. A visit to any animal shelter will reveal the cold, harsh truth about human compassion. But there is no question that domesticated animals have, as entire species, benefited significantly through their relationships with us. The Bengal tiger is on the brink of extinction, while its small cousin, *Felis catus*, has spread across the globe by partnering with our species. Likewise, the most successful subspecies of *Canis lupus*, the subspecies that overshadows all others in both range and population, is *Canis lupus familiaris*—the wolf that decided to become humankind's familiar spirit, the domestic dog.

Some animals are so vastly different from us that we cannot develop any kind of familiar relationship with them. It is difficult to imagine having a relationship with a clam! Some invertebrates do make interesting pets, but it is their alien nature rather than their familiarity that provides much of the interest. Dogs, on the other hand, demand a familiar interaction with us.

Between these extremes—the dog and the invertebrates—whether a pet of any species is a familiar spirit is largely dependent on whether or not you choose to develop a personal relationship with the animal. Again, this is easier to do with some species than with others. Cats are usually very accepting of an affectionate relationship, although they certainly do not require it. The dog, however, especially if acquired as a young puppy, needs that familiar relationship if it is to integrate itself into the human household.

DOGS

It seems fitting that *familiaris* is part of the dog's scientific name, being the species that almost demands a familiar relationship. With a dog, you cannot just dump some food into a bowl or in a cage once a day and then forget about the animal. Not if you have anything vaguely resembling a soul.

To the best of my knowledge, a mixed-breed bitch named Sasha was the first nonhuman to have an active role in an Ár nDraíocht Féin (ADF) ritual. It was not an official ADF ritual, which is always open to the public; this was a private wedding, but both the bride and the groom were ADF druids, and the wedding closely followed ADF's core order of ritual.

During the wedding, the bride and groom asked for the blessings of the three spirit kindred: the gods, the ancestors, and the worldly spirits. First, they took turns addressing their respective patron deities, each giving an offering at the altar as they did so. After this, they asked for the blessings of their ancestors. In turn, the bride and groom approached their families, thanked them for all they had received, and then asked their ancestors to guide them as they entered into a union with each another.

The officiant then asked if there was anyone who could speak for the spirits of this world. A young man came forward with the groom's dog, Sasha, at his side. Sasha wore a garland of roses around her neck, and she sat politely after the young man led her up to the groom and his bride. She had been prepared for this moment over the previous several months. When the officiant asked for a blessing, Sasha was supposed to lift up her paw.

The officiant looked down at the dog and said, "Sasha, on behalf of those who have no voice, what say you now?"

Sasha not only lifted her paw, she accompanied the gesture with a quick and enthusiastic bark! Fifty years from now, few people who attended the wedding are going to remember the vows that the couple exchanged that afternoon, but they will almost surely remember the dog who gave its blessing!

Did Sasha know what was going on around her? Some people will say she did not, but I beg to differ. Sure, the subtle nuances of the ritual held no meaning for her, but in her own doggy way, Sasha knew that something special was happening—something that focused everyone's attention on her master and the female whom he was so very fond of. Sasha knew that she was being included in this special moment. She knew what was expected (lifting her paw), and she performed the gesture so gracefully, with such practiced perfection, that she could not hold in the proud bark. She truly did convey the blessings of the worldly spirits, because Sasha, like every animal, is very much a spirit of this world.

Folklore describes a variety of dog spirits, from the Celtic *cu sith* to grims, yeth hounds, and Gally-trots (Briggs, p. 140). These "fairy dogs" have different coat colors and a different general appearance, but they are never toy breeds; most are described instead as exceptionally large. Some of them are benevolent and some malevolent, but, no matter their intentions, they are almost always intimidating in some way.

Most fairy dogs are either solid black or pure white, although, as with mortal dogs, the coat color does not seem to have any relationship to their behavior. A notable exception is the cu sith (pronounced "coo-shee") of the Scottish Highlands, which has a shaggy, dark green coat. Folklore tells of the cu sith accompanying Scottish fairies on their hunts and guarding their homes. They are sometimes allowed by the fairies to wander loose, and these large green dogs can be dangerous if encountered.

The grim takes the form of a large black dog. *Grim* is another name for the god Woden, and I do not think it too much of a stretch to surmise that grims answer to him. The grim is often, but not always, the spirit guardian of a burial ground. In Christian times, these black fairy dogs became known as church grims due to their habit of guarding the graves in churchyards. In Sweden, the same beast is known as the Kirkegrimm. A grim known as the Black Dog of Newgate was said to go to the window of a dying person and howl to indicate that the person would soon die. Grims are usually associated with the dead in some way, so they are often feared although they are not really evil. In Yorkshire, the grim would leave the churchyard and wander around the countryside in stormy weather (Simpson and Roud, p. 156).

Yeth hounds, or yell hounds, are another breed of spirit dog that may have close ties with Woden. These headless dogs travel in packs with a huntsman who is said, in the Christian era, to be the Devil. As Katharine Briggs points out in *An Encyclopedia of Fairies* (p. 314), it was not uncommon for Christian folklore to portray Pagan gods as "devils." In this case, the god would be Woden. Yeth hounds are unusual in that they are headless. Elsewhere in folklore, the dogs in Woden's Wild Hunt are described as having "hideous eyes" (which strongly suggests that, unlike yeth hounds, they also have heads). The dogs' heads (or lack thereof) in the wild hunt seem to be their most variable feature. In Lancashire, these dogs were called Gabriel Hounds, and were notable for their human heads.

The Gally-trot is a huge, shaggy white dog. It is said that the Gally-trot will chase after anyone who runs from it, which would be more astounding were it not for the fact that almost every mortal dog will do the exact same thing! It is a fact of life that dogs chase things. To be fair, the Gally-trot is as large as a steer, so being chased by one would be considerably more frightening than being chased by your average terrier.

As a totem animal, the dog represents both protection and faithfulness (Andrews, p. 264). It should come as no surprise then that dogs are often associated with gods of healing, such as Nodens and Asclepius.

No animal is better than the dog at establishing a familiar relationship with us. Like us, the dog is a tribal creature. It has a strong desire to have a safe and secure position in a pack, even if that pack consists of nobody but the dog and you. But as with other tribal commitments, this is not a relationship to enter into frivolously. A new puppy can be as demanding as a child. It has a lot to learn, and no one but yourself to teach it. Furthermore, it represents a commitment that will consume the next ten to fifteen years of your life. If you do not think this is a long time, consider where you were ten years ago today.

Dogs are brilliant animals, but I am consistently amazed by people who seem to think a puppy is vastly more intelligent than a human being. Time and again, I hear of somebody who has brought home a new puppy, thrown some newspapers on the floor, and then left for work or school. The story always ends the same way. This person returns home and is startled to discover that the puppy had no idea what the newspaper was for. This is akin to expecting a human child to instinctively know how to use a potty chair without any training!

If you think you want a dog for a familiar, you need to first make sure that you understand its needs. Ask yourself the following questions:

- Can you devote most of your time to the dog for the first week after you have brought it into your home? This is especially important for puppies, but a dog of any age needs help learning the household rules.

- After that first week, can you devote some time *every single day* to the dog? I am not talking about dumping some food into a bowl; the dog needs to interact with you. This can be a walk, a game of fetch, or just about any other activity, so long as both you and the dog are involved with each other.

• Do you have sufficient living accommodations for the dog? A dog of medium size or larger needs a fenced yard unless you intend to take it on several long walks each day.

• Can you afford the medical bills? There will be shots and preventative pills, not to mention the possibility of a medical emergency that could cost hundreds or even thousands of dollars.

• Do you have experience with dogs, and, if not, are you willing to attend obedience classes with your dog? A good obedience class is for the benefit of the owner as much as for the dog, and you should attend one if you have not already kept dogs in your household successfully.

If you answer no to any of these questions, you should probably consider an animal other than a dog. A dog will be thoroughly committed to you—which is why they make such great familiars—but this means you need to be equally committed to the dog, and that is not a lifestyle that works for everybody.

Deciding that you do want a dog immediately leads to more questions, and to answer them you need to be honest with yourself. Do you care what other people think? When it comes to dogs, everyone has an opinion and 90 percent of those opinions are founded firmly on ignorance. For some reason, a lot of people equate the value of a dog with its bulk; large dogs like Rottweilers and Great Danes are "cool," while the toy breeds are "not cool." You may not cling to this prejudice, but you should be aware that other people do. In other words, if you are insecure about your masculinity, a Pomeranian probably is not the breed for you. Only secure, confident men should own Pomeranians. (This is rarely an issue for women.)

There is much to be said for choosing a toy breed. They are great for urban dwellers. I can tell you from personal experience that it is far easier to rent an apartment if you have an eight-pound dog than if you have an eighty-pound dog. A smaller dog is less expensive to feed, less expensive to medicate, and much easier to carry to the car if it has a seizure and you need to rush it to the emergency veterinary office at three in the morning. Any problem you can have with a dog is directly proportionate to its size, which is why many toy dogs are poorly trained. If little Fifi tinkles on the living room carpet, it is probably because her "mommy" really does not mind all that much. That sort of thing would simply not be tolerated if Fifi were a Saint Bernard! The truth is, a toy dog can be taught to behave as well as any larger breed. If you do not believe me, attend an obedience show where you can see Chihuahuas, Yorkies, and Toy Poodles do amazing things in the ring.

What about hair? Do you enjoy combing and primping and grooming? If not, avoid a breed that requires this. A well-groomed Yorkshire Terrier is a beautiful animal, but its beauty is the result of constant care. Professional grooming is an option, but it is also an additional expense, which may or may not be an issue for you.

Activity level is another important consideration. If you are not an athletic person, avoid athletic breeds like the Siberian Husky, the Australian Shepherd, or the Whippet. These are wonderful animals, but they are not going to be content lying in front of the television all day. (I know somebody is going to protest that his Whippet does nothing but watch soap operas. There is always an exception to the rule.)

If you want the dog to be your familiar spirit—if you honestly want to develop and nurture that *familiar* relationship—your best choice is an animal with a personality and needs similar to your own. What the dog looks like should be your very last consideration. It does not matter that you like the appearance of a Bullmastiff if that breed is not compatible with your needs. Do your research, and let appearance enter into the equation only after you have narrowed down your search to two or three breeds.

Likewise, Pagans can be tempted to select dogs based on cultural origin, but this is a mistake. A Saluki is not the best dog for every Kemetic Pagan, nor is the Irish Wolfhound a good choice for every Celt. Cultural origin ranks way down there with appearance when it comes to choosing a breed.

What about a mixed breed? The advantage of a mixed breed is that the dog will be (or should be) much less expensive than a purebred dog. The disadvantage is that you do not know what you are getting. Even a designer dog can be a genetic grab bag.

Unlike the designer dog, which is the intentional cross of two known breeds, most mixed-breed dogs are of dubious parentage. This is even more of a grab bag. The dog might be referred to as a Collie-mix or a Beagle-mix, and the "mix" suffix means that nobody has any idea who the father was.

It is extremely important to know exactly what you want in a dog if you are considering a mixed breed, because the physical and temperamental traits will not be clearly laid out for you the way they are with a purebred dog. Try to spend some time with the animal, alone, away from any littermates and preferably from any distractions. Does the animal *feel* like a familiar spirit? Does the dog pay attention to you? If it is a puppy, pick it up and hold it on its back, as you would a baby. Puppies will almost always object to this at first, but it should calm down after a few seconds if it trusts you as a familiar should.

I highly recommend that you obtain your dog from a breeder (if a purebred) or a shelter (if a mixed breed). The worst place you can get a dog is from a pet shop. The best pet shops are aware of this and no longer sell puppies at all. In stores where puppies are still sold, no matter what the salesperson tells you, it is highly unlikely that the puppy in the window came from a reputable breeder. Responsible breeders who care about their dogs simply do not permit their puppies to be displayed in shop cages for passersby to gawk at. The puppy in the window probably came from a puppy mill, where adult dogs are kept in miserable conditions for the sole purpose of producing live "merchandise."

When you go directly to a breeder, you have the opportunity to meet the puppy's mother. (If the mother is not on the premises, leave immediately. Something is amiss.) The father may or may not be present, but your puppy should still be with its mom. The breeder should be willing to answer any questions you may have and, ideally, will ask *you* a few questions. Good breeders want to know something about who is taking their puppies. Do not be offended if the breeder asks about your home, how many hours a day you will be gone, and so on. These questions are evidence that the breeder has the puppy's best interest at heart. It means your puppy was bred by someone who cared very much about it.

If you go to a shelter, you should also ask questions and expect reasonable answers. A good shelter will tell you everything known about the dog's history, and should let you spend some time alone with the animal before you make a decision. After all, they do not want you to bring the dog back, so it is in their own best interest to match you with an animal that you will enjoy living with.

It is a compassionate gesture to adopt a shelter dog, but you must be even more careful in your choice if you intend the animal to become your familiar spirit. With the exception of newborn puppies, every shelter dog has a history, and it may take months or even years for a dog that has been tormented and abused to enter into a familiar relationship with any human being. It is not my intention to discourage anyone from adopting a dog from a shelter. A shelter dog can and should become a great companion, but the odds of this happening will be greater if you choose the animal carefully and learn as much as you can about it before bringing it home.

The sixteenth-century witch's familiar, regardless of species, was tamed by feeding it milk, chicken, or bread (Margaret Murray, p. 84). I question how effective this is with toads, which, in my experience, take very little interest in bread, but it is certainly the best way to initiate a familiar relationship with your dog! Food is a universal language, signifying comfort. Professional dog trainers always use food as a part of their process. Food is a means of communicating to your dog that you are a source of security and fulfillment.

Unfortunately, most people feed their dogs with the same disinterest that they refuel their automobiles. The typical dog owner fills a bowl with dry kibble and leaves it on the floor all day. Thus the food has no meaning.

Begin feeding your dog immediately when you first bring it home, but not in a bowl. Sit before your household altar with your dog next to you. Take a bit of food and offer it to the dog with your fingers. Speak the dog's name, praise the dog when it takes the food, and then give it another small piece. If the dog snaps at your fingers, do not scold it; simply remove the food. Only allow the dog to have the food when taking it gently from your hand.

Look at everything that is happening as you do this. The dog is learning its name. It is learning that sitting quietly beside you at the altar is a good thing. It is learning that you are the source of good things (food). It is learning that good things are more accessible when taken politely. In essence, it is learning to have a comfortable, familiar relationship with you.

After a few days of this, your dog should be ready for its first short ritual. Have a small piece of food that can be easily divided and that both you and your dog will enjoy. A piece of chicken or cheese works well for this, or a small piece of bread if you are vegan.

In this ritual, you will be presenting your new familiar to a deity. If you already have a close connection with a god or goddess, addressing that deity is entirely appropriate. Otherwise, direct your words to a deity within your cultural pantheon who has an affinity for the canine spirit. Here are some examples:

Culture	Deity
Anglo-Saxon	Woden
British	Nodens
Egyptian	Anubis
Hellenic (Greek)	Artemis or Asclepius
Irish	Lugh
Norse	Odin
Roman	Diana
Sumerian	Bau
Welsh	Gwyn ap Nudd

You should embellish the ritual with the words, symbols, gestures, and actions that are culturally appropriate for your spiritual orientation. As a Saxon Pagan, I would begin by carrying fire around the perimeter of the ritual area while asking Thunor to bless and sanctify everything within that space. Then I would offer some ale or mead to Woden, pouring it as a libation.

A Hellenic Pagan would begin by washing his or her hands, kindling a fire on the altar, and offering an opening prayer to the goddess Hestia before directly addressing Artemis (or Asclepius).

Once you have created a sacred space that reflects your spiritual paradigm, and have your dog sitting or lying calmly at your side, say to the deity:

(Name of deity), behold this familiar spirit.
Look well upon this fair creature who I name
(Name of familiar).
Grant me the wisdom to know his/her mind
and the compassion to know his/her spirit
that I might honor you with greater
strength and understanding.

Now take the food you have brought to the ritual and tear it into two pieces. Say:

Fur and skin,
the same within.
By moon and by sun,
the two are made one.

Give one piece of the food to your dog and eat the other piece at the same time. Try to look into your dog's eyes as both of you take in the same food, as you take in the same essence. Eye contact is good if it is natural and voluntary, but do not force the dog to meet your gaze. For a dog, forced eye contact is a threatening action.

You may spend a few minutes in quiet contemplation with your familiar, but do not extend this for too long. This should be a positive experience for both of you, so bring the ritual to its conclusion before the animal loses interest. Finish by closing the circle, or thanking the kindred, or giving a piacular offering—whatever is appropriate for your spiritual path.

Just as you establish a cycle of reciprocity when giving an offering to the gods, you can nurture a similar cycle with a canine familiar every time you offer it food. After your dog has learned "sit," ask it to do so when you are preparing its meal. The dog should sit and remain sitting until you have placed the bowl on the floor (or in its stand). There is nothing cruel or even particularly demanding in expecting your dog to wait politely. If the dog gets out of the sitting position, immediately stop preparing its food. If it does not immediately sit again (and most dogs do catch on to this quite rapidly), gently say "sit" as a reminder. The dog will very likely leave the sitting position as you begin to place its bowl on the floor. When this happens, just stand up again with the bowl and wait until the dog returns to a sit. Within several days—if not sooner—your dog will wait patiently until *you* say it is all right to begin eating.

This is not an idle exercise. Again, look at what is happening. The dog is learning that lunging and grabbing is not necessarily an effective way of getting what it wants. It is learning that pleasing you (by sitting) will be rewarded. It is learning to pay attention to you, which is fundamental to the deep, familiar relationship that you can build with a dog.

While we are on the subject of food, I should mention the importance of providing your canine familiar with a healthy diet. The least expensive kibble is not necessarily a bargain if it leads to expensive veterinary care later in the dog's life. And do not trust the blurb on the bag saying how great the stuff is for your dog. Look up and down the aisle where these bags are displayed; there are no bags anywhere with a label saying, "Contains an Unhealthy Blend of Cheap Filler." The front of the bag always suggests a product that will deliver great taste and nutrition. You have to read the small print to find out what is actually inside, and even then it may remain a mystery. Give special attention to the first three or four ingredients listed, as these are the primary ingredients in the food.

Many dogs have or may develop an allergy to grains like corn, wheat, and soy. If your dog has chronic skin or ear infections, check to see whether these grains are in the food you buy.

I no longer feed commercial foods to my dogs. By preparing their food myself, I know exactly what they are eating. I do not need to scrutinize ingredient labels or worry about the quality of those ingredients.

If you want to provide whole, natural foods for your canine familiar, be sure to educate yourself about the foods that are toxic for their species. The most common of these are chocolate, grapes (including raisins), onions, garlic, uncooked dough, and raw eggs. Also be aware that your dog is likely to temporarily experience gas or diarrhea when you first offer real food if the animal is accustomed to a diet of kibble or canned dog food. This reaction is entirely natural. If you were to eat nothing but fast food for months on end, your own body would react to the change of a healthy salad.

There are cookbooks written specifically for dogs, and it can be fun to try different recipes. Over the years I have come up with my own recipe that is both healthful and easy to prepare.

Alaric's Canine Cuisine

- 3 pounds of turkey, chicken, or lean beef (varies with whatever is on sale)
- 2 pounds carrots

- 3–5 yams
- 2 cups water
- 1 cup organic brown rice
- 1–2 zucchini or yellow squash
- 2 cans peas (preferably low salt or salt free)
- ½ cup vegetable oil

Cook the meat. How you do this depends on what you have bought. Cook ground turkey or ground beef in a skillet. Cook chicken breasts in the oven. (There are many people who recommend raw foods. The raw-versus-cooked argument has persisted for years. I cook the meats that I feed my dogs, and this has worked very well for me.)

While the meat is cooking, chop the carrots and yams into bite-size pieces. How big these are depends on your dog. A Great Dane's bite size is considerably larger than a Shih Tzu's bite size.

Put 2 cups of water into a large pot. Add the chopped carrots and yams, plus the rice. Cook this over medium heat for 45 minutes, stirring occasionally.

While the veggies are cooking, cut the meat into bite-size pieces. Obviously you do not need to do this if you have used ground meat.

Cut up the zucchini or yellow squash, and add this to the veggies after they have cooked for 45 minutes. Also add the 2 cans of peas. Let this cook another 15 minutes, stirring more frequently to avoid scorching.

Mix together the veggie mix and the cooked meats. This is much easier to do if you let both cool down a little. After mixing these together, add the vegetable oil.

How much to feed your dog depends on how large and active it is. As a very rough guideline, start out feeding ½ cup daily for every five pounds of body weight up to twenty-five pounds. For larger dogs, give 1 cup daily for every fifteen pounds of body weight. Then keep an eye on your dog (which you should be doing anyway). If the dog loses weight to a point where you begin to see its ribs, then increase the amount of food. If the dog begins to get fat, decrease the amount.

This is a book about getting in touch with your spirituality, not about animal care, so we do not have room here to discuss housebreaking, crate training, problem behaviors, and other issues that are better addressed elsewhere. I highly recommend obedience classes, especially if you have never had a dog before, but also if sharing your life with a canine familiar is second nature to you. Group obedience classes are excellent opportunities to enjoy quality time with your new companion.

CATS

What if you are not up to meeting the demands that a dog will present? What if you want a familiar that is reasonably responsive but requires a minimum of fuss? If you do not care whether the familiar will come when you call it or take a walk with you through the woods, you might be better off with a cat.

As a familiar, the witch's cat has become a cliché, although not without good reason. There is a mystique about the cat that has given rise to all sorts of beliefs and superstitions, often contradictory. In the United States, a black cat is supposed to be a portent of bad fortune, while in England it is a bringer of luck (Simpson and Roud, p. 49). Good luck and misfortune are both associated with almost everything about the cat: its color, its behavior, and even the month it was born.

Historically, the cat has often suffered unfairly from human prejudice. Cats were treated brutally during the witch hunts, and at other times were believed to be natural thieves (Hartley, p. 125). The latter may have some truth to it, but almost any animal—including humans—will sometimes steal given the right circumstances.

There are not many references to fairy cats in folklore, but perhaps this is because every cat has some fairy connection with mystery and magic. Instead, in the lore of the cat, this animal is more likely to be associated with a deity, such as the Egyptian goddess Bast, the Scandinavians' Freya, or the Hindu goddess Shashthi (Andrews, p. 258).

Cats first attained their place as familiar spirits in Egypt, where they were valued for their ability to control mice and rats. They were greatly loved, and those who could afford to do so would have their cats embalmed and mummified after they died. More than 300,000 mummified cats were found in one temple to Bast when it was excavated and explored.

As a familiar, the cat has one enormous advantage over the dog, and that is its ease of care. It is not a tribal or pack animal. Instead, the cat is a solitary hunter, and for this reason it can get along very well without our immediate presence. Leave out enough food, and the cat can usually be left alone for a weekend without suffering any ill effects. Most of the Pagans

I've known who have cats are comfortable leaving their animals alone for a couple of days.

Most, but not all. Laisey Hahn, a Pagan woman from Minnesota, believes her cats should have more constant attention. "I would never leave cat food out for a whole weekend and leave them—at most an overnight trip," she says. "And I wouldn't leave out food. Kibble is very bad for kitties; cats need more water in their diet than they naturally have the inclination to drink. A diet of dry food only can lead to significant kidney problems."

Training is not as much of an issue for cats as it is for dogs. The cat, descended from desert hunters, has an instinct to bury its strongly scented waste in sand, so "housebreaking" usually consists of nothing more than showing the cat where the litter box is located. And further training is rarely an option that most people consider. Again, this is not universal. Laisey also tells me, "Most people have this idea that cats can't be trained and therefore they don't try. I bought a cat training book last year and have been training Frida to do simple things like stand up, jump from chair to chair, et cetera. Of course it only works if I bribe her with treats!"

As with dogs, training a cat is more than an exercise in control. It is a means of bonding with the animal and developing a deeper, more familiar relationship. The good news, for cat owners, is that training is an option rather than a necessity. An untrained cat is not as likely to eat your favorite pair of shoes when you leave the animal alone for the afternoon.

Cats do come in a great variety of breeds, but this, too, is a less important consideration than it is for a dog. Different feline breeds vary less in both size and temperament than dog breeds. If you choose a kitten for your familiar, most likely the animal will not be purebred simply because selective breeding is less common for cats. The owner of the kitten's mother probably will not know what male cat sired the litter. This only matters if you personally want a purebred animal. Unlike dog breeds, most cat breeds were not developed to perform specific tasks such as herding cattle or hunting vermin. With a few exceptions, the behavior of one breed of cat is similar to that of most others.

Still, when considering a specific breed, educate yourself about its typical personality and needs. The Siamese, for example, tends to be a very vocal cat with a greater than average need for attention. This breed is usually not a good choice if you are gone most of the day or if you want a quiet familiar. Keep in mind, too, that long-haired breeds like the Persian or Balinese require frequent grooming to maintain those luxurious coats.

Also, just as with a dog, it is always better to adopt a cat or acquire one directly from the breeder rather than purchasing it at a pet shop. If you are not particular about the breed, your new cat may cost you nothing at all. Due to irresponsible breeding, there are always more kittens available than homes to adopt them. On the other hand, the nominal adoption fees charged by most no-kill shelters support these worthy organizations and should not dissuade you from adopting a shelter cat.

As a rule, food rewards often mean less to a cat than to a dog. If your cat familiar is motivated by treats, count yourself lucky. If not, do not force the issue. In exchange for not making nearly so many demands as a dog, the cat will often be uncooperative in responding to your own demands. Cat people call this "independence."

You can, however, establish a more familiar relationship with a cat than with many other animals. If you and your cat enjoy any similar food (tuna fish often works), you can present your new familiar to either your patron deity or to a deity within your cultural pantheon who has an affinity for the feline spirit. Here are some examples:

Culture	Deity
Anglo-Saxon	Fréo
British	Britannia
Egyptian	Bast
Hellenic (Greek)	Artemis
Norse	Freya
Roman	Diana

I am not aware of any Irish, Welsh, or Sumerian deities associated specifically with cats. If you follow one of these spiritual paths, address whichever deity you have the closest relationship with. The ritual itself is exactly what you would do with a dog.

You can acknowledge your cat as your familiar with this ritual even if it does not respond especially well to treats. Instead of offering food, simply hold the cat close as you sit before the altar and address the deity. Hold it against your chest and feel your own aura merge with your cat's as you say the words, "Fur and skin, the same within." This body aura was known to the Saxons as the *hama*. Let that part of you, the protective field that surrounds your physical body, flow into the cat's hama.

It is nicer if you can include the sharing of food as a part of the ritual, but with cats you are never completely in control.

Most Pagans incorporate meditation as part of their spiritual practice, and a feline familiar can be an excellent help in this respect. To receive any real benefit, you will need to first develop that essential "familiar" relationship with the animal. Your bond with the cat must be strong enough that it will consent to sit on your lap or beside you throughout the meditation. (A well-mannered canine familiar, if you have one, can also do this with only a little training.) There are different techniques for meditating, but whatever you ordinarily do is fine as long as you can do it with your familiar sitting close.

If you are going to light candles, burn incense, cast a magic circle, or anything similar, do this early to give your cat plenty of time to accept the changes in its environment. From the cat's perspective, it owns everything in its immediate vicinity, including you. A cat will often want to investigate any alterations in its surroundings before it is willing to settle down and assist with your meditation.

As you begin meditating, slowly stroke the cat (or dog) with gentle, relaxed motions. Be aware of the cat, but do not allow your awareness to distract you from your meditation. Petting or stroking a companion animal can help lower blood pressure and reduce stress. These same measurable effects are induced through meditation, so it is easy to see how one activity nurtures the other. The intentional interaction with your familiar will help bring you into a meditative state of being.

It should go without saying that you must never attempt to force your familiar into participating in meditations or any kind of daily devotion. Nobody has ever entered a meditative state while wrestling a cat. This is why it is imperative that you accustom your cat to sitting quietly next to you as you stroke it before making any attempt at meditating with the animal.

Cooperation only goes so far with an animal that evolved as a solitary hunter. No matter how well behaved your feline familiar is, there will probably be times when it will decide halfway through your meditation that it is finished for the day. The cat will drop down from the chair or sofa and walk off to investigate something it finds far more interesting than you. Acknowledge this, and continue with your meditation. If you have developed even a moderate level of mental discipline, this should not be difficult for you. Part of working with a cat as a familiar is accepting its independent nature.

Pagan author Deborah Blake (*Everyday Witch Book of Rituals*) says, "I have found with cats that they participate on their own terms. Most of my cats show very little interest in my magical work." Deborah has five cats, and the exception to this general rule is a black cat named, appropriately enough, Magic. "When my coven is practicing inside in my living room (my cats don't go outside), we have an altar table that we all stand around," says Deborah. "As soon as we get started, Magic strolls into the room and walks around the circle deosil (clockwise) every single time. Then she either sits under the table, continues to meander around the circle, or perches herself on the sofa and supervises from there."

Deborah's cat Magic also joins her at other times. "I also have a daily practice of greeting the gods first thing in the morning and asking for their help with my day, and saying thank you at the end of the day," she tells me. "I do both of these while lying in bed. Magic almost always comes and lies by my head while I do this, purring madly."

When it comes to magical and spiritual work, Deborah says of her cat, "I believe that her presence adds something important." This is something I have heard time and again when talking with people who have cat familiars. Although the cat is more aloof, it seems to offer something—some influence—to those in its proximity who share a familiar relationship with it.

Joy Bennett shares her Midwestern home with four cats, and also believes the cat can add something important, if intangible, to rituals. "They have a calming, soothing influence," says Joy. "I find them especially effective for healing. When I am sick, I get Pyewackett—he's the best for this—and hold him close to me." All of Joy's cats are rescues, homeless cats who needed, and found, a loving environment. The healing relationship between cat and human flows both ways at the Bennett house. Joy's husband, Jack, collects the cats' shed claw sheaths whenever he finds them. Why? For a sort of veterinary magic. "A cat's sheath is no different than a human fingernail," Jack says. "It's a link with the animal. When one of the cats is sick (although it also gets a visit to the veterinarian's office), I use the sheaths to work healing magic. I don't know which sheaths came from which cats, but it's just a general vitality spell, so all of the cats benefit, including the one most needing that energy."

As I said earlier, a cat usually will not respond to food rewards with the same enthusiasm that a dog will. A dog will almost always take an interest in treats (although some are more responsive to food than others), but a cat has a different metabolism. It is natural for the cat to eat less frequently, and so it may sometimes refuse not only treats but even its dinner (Pitcairn, p. 47). Nevertheless, a healthy diet is just as essential for a cat if you hope to develop a strong, familiar relationship with the animal. Your cat will respond better to you. The cat's dietary needs are different than a dog's. We tend to lump animals into general categories of carnivore, herbivore, and omnivore, but life is far more diverse than this. While dogs are indeed carnivores, most of them will enjoy an occasional fruit or vegetable tidbit, and my own recipe for Chien Cuisine given earlier in this chapter includes yams, squash, carrots, peas, and rice. Cats require a higher percentage of protein, and have dietary needs requiring meats or meat byproducts (Pitcairn, p. 52). If you feed your familiar a commercial cat food, read the ingredient label carefully and make sure the primary ingredients—those listed first on the label—are meats and organs. And as with commercial dog food, the meat should be specified: chicken, turkey, beef, or whatever. Listing an ingredient generically as "meat" is as meaningless as saying there is "food" in the food. Laisey Hahn points out that "real meat is always better than the mysterious 'meat byproduct,' and there are now even grain-free canned foods on the market which are also better for their health."

You can, of course, prepare food yourself for the cat familiar. Although more difficult to find than the canine equivalent, there are cookbooks specifically for cats. In *Dr. Pitcairn's Com-*

plete Guide to Natural Health for Dogs and Cats, Dr. Pitcairn gives a variety of recipes for dishes. Although a cat familiar is less likely than a dog to overeat, it is always a good idea to keep an eye on its weight (pp. 38–39).

OTHER FAMILIARS

Part of the appeal of a dog or a cat as a familiar is that the animal can roam about the house freely, with minimal supervision.

Margaret Murray mentions people in the sixteenth century keeping smaller familiars in pots and boxes (p. 84), but today it is customary to keep them in specially designed cages. Small mammals, birds, and reptiles must be confined for their own safety if for no other reason. When these animals can be supervised, it is possible to release them from their quarters for limited periods of time, and some can become suitable familiars for people with enough patience to work with them.

Some of the small animals suitable as familiars are rodents, an order of mammals that we humans have, historically, had a predominantly adversarial relationship with. Rodents enjoy the same foods that we enjoy, and will steal our stored food as casually as we steal honey from bees and milk from cattle. Worse, wild rodents are capable of transmitting a bewildering array of human diseases. They do not spread these diseases intentionally, but that was no comfort to the millions of men, women, and children who died from the Black Plague in fourteenth-century Europe.

The good news is that a domesticated, captive-born rodent is no more likely to carry a deadly disease than your next-door neighbor is. The food thing is another issue altogether, creating one very real need for a cage.

When people think of rodents as companion animals, the first species that come to mind are usually hamsters and gerbils. I would not dissuade you from trying to develop a familiar relationship with one of these small creatures if you feel some special affinity for them. I have kept both hamsters and gerbils and have loved both, but in my opinion they are poorly suited to be familiars as a general rule. Both hamsters and gerbils tend to be skittish even when tamed. The hamster is nocturnal, which means it will want to sleep when you want to interact with it, unless you work a night shift. And a sleepy, annoyed hamster is liable to bite. If I had to choose between a hamster and a gerbil, my choice would be the latter, but among the order of rodents, both of these would be near the bottom of my list.

What would be at the top of my list? The domestic rat. EWWWWW!!!

If this is your initial reaction, I understand completely. I once shared this common prejudice. Even the word *rat*, when applied to a human being, means the worst sort of scoundrel. Rats were a primary factor in the spread of the aforementioned Black Plague, and they have caused unimaginable damage to humankind's food supplies for centuries. The wild black rat (*Rattus rattus*) and Norwegian or brown rat (*Rattus norvegicus*) are aggressive and potentially dangerous, especially for small children and the elderly, and these are the species that live with or near us humans in their wild state. It is little wonder that so many people have a strong aversion not only to black and Norwegian rats but also to their domestic cousins.

My own prejudice melted away long ago, back when I was still a high school student. To earn extra spending money, I would often house-sit for neighboring families when they went on vacation. A family down the street had asked me to drop by their house two or three times every day to check on their pets. When I stopped in to find out exactly what my duties would be, I learned that there would be three pets in my care: a mixed-breed dog named Moby, a parakeet named Fletcher... and a large male rat named Henry.

While I was talking to the wife, I glanced over at Henry's cage. Henry yawned. Henry had enormous teeth. I came very close to telling the woman that I would not be able to look in on these family pets, but then her daughter, a girl of no more than six or seven, went over to Henry's cage and took him out. She held the big, nasty rat close to her chest and stroked his back. Watching the little girl, I realized that I could not back out of this job. Not if I wanted to retain even a trace of self-respect.

During the week that Moby, Fletcher, and Henry were in my care, my prejudice toward the rat gradually transformed into trust, and even into a small degree of affection. Henry was a gentle creature who never once attempted to bite me.

Domestic rats, also called "fancy rats," were bred from the Norwegian brown rat, but share little in common with their ancestors other than their general form. When treated well, the fancy rat usually has a sweet disposition and can readily become attached to a specific human or humans. They react less to sudden lights and sounds than wild rats do, and they are indeed "fancy," with different colors and markings. The Dumbo breed has large, round ears that sit at the sides of its head. The Manx breed is tailless. Himalayan rats are white, with markings similar to those on Siamese cats.

It was some years later that I had a rat of my own, which became my familiar. He was a black-hooded rat that I named Demetrius. By "hooded" I mean that his coat was white, with a black head and patch that extended down his back. Demetrius stayed in a cage when I had to leave him alone, but otherwise he would usually sit happily on my shoulder as I went about my business. He even went to a few parties with me, riding on my shoulder and enjoying corn chips and similar snacks that the other guests would offer him.

If I could not have a dog, my second choice would almost certainly be a rat. Few animals are as responsive as this under-appreciated species. They are amazingly intelligent.

As a familiar, the rat is nevertheless a rodent. It will not interact as completely or as reliably as a well-behaved dog, of course, but, once tamed, it can participate in the meditation exercise described earlier. I have found it easier to develop a familiar relationship with the male rat than with the female, but that could be a personal quirk of mine.

No medieval witch ever had a guinea pig as a familiar because the species was not even introduced to Europe until the sixteenth century, but this is another relatively calm rodent to consider if you want a small mammal. Like the rat, the guinea pig is an intelligent creature. Its worst traits, in my opinion, are how easily it is startled and the amount of noise it makes, the latter only being a problem if you live in an apartment or prefer a quiet environment. Guinea pigs are much more vocal than other rodents, communicating with each other (and you) by whistling, chirping, squealing, and purring. They are happier if kept in pairs or small groups. Domesticated guinea pigs come in different breeds with both long and short coats. Unless you actually want a familiar that requires constant brushing, I recommend the short-coat breeds.

When socialized correctly, a guinea pig enjoys being picked up and held, so it can become just as suitable a familiar as a dog, cat, or rat.

Just as there are fancy rats, there are also fancy mice, and these domesticated animals share no more in common with their ancestor, the common house mouse (*Mus musculus*), than the domestic rat shares with the Norwegian brown rat. Compared to a domestic rat, the mouse tends to be more skittish and, in my opinion, less intelligent. Mice are also relatively short-lived, rarely enjoying a life span of more than two years. The advantage of mice is their small size, which can be a significant consideration for people with extremely limited personal space. Males tend to have a strong odor and do not usually coexist well with other males, but their personalities can be more entertaining.

It is understandable that a creature as tiny as a mouse is innately terrified of being handled by an enormous human. Taming the mouse can be more difficult than with other rodents. It is not impossible, but even so, a rat will prove to be much more tractable as a familiar.

Rabbits are not rodents, they are lagomorphs, but people often lump them in the same category, and they can certainly be as potentially destructive as wild rodents. Rabbits that have been introduced into Australia and New Zealand, where they have few natural predators other than humans, have become serious pests. But few people have the aversion to rabbits that so many of us exhibit toward rats and mice. Perhaps this is due in part to fictional characters like Peter Rabbit, the White Rabbit of Lewis Carroll's Wonderland, or the animated Bugs Bunny. In the popular imagination, rabbits are cute.

I do not know anyone personally who includes a rabbit actively in spiritual or magical work, but I suspect these animals could make very good familiars for the right people. In the 1980s and 1990s, more families began keeping rabbits indoors, where they can be trained to use a litter box. The rabbit's need to chew should be taken into consideration, and I do not think it is a good idea to leave one of these animals unsupervised for long periods of time. Rabbits can also deliver nasty, potentially dangerous kicks with their hind legs.

Your choice of familiar is not restricted to mammals. Devin Hunter, host of Internet radio's *The Modern Witch*, lives in San Francisco and has a feathered familiar by the name of Sophia. She is a ring-necked dove. As a familiar, Sophia has proven to be a source of spiritual strength for Devin. He says that "in times of great stress, I will simply hold her, meditate, trance, or chant and connect to my form of divinity. Sophia is a Greek word for wisdom, and it is said that Sophia (Wisdom) came to earth in the form of a dove. As such, I connect with the higher self and its wisdom while working with my dove in meditative forms."

Here we see an avian familiar, a dove, being used in meditation in a similar way as any tame and well-behaved mammal might be. Devin is a male witch, and Sophia also helps him with his magical workings. He tells me, "I have used her to send messages to loved ones; messages of love, hope, peace, and freedom. I generally will hold her and, while in circle, talk to her, enchanting her with each whisper or stroke, and then will let her fly around in circle a bit. I place her back in her cage when the work has been done."

Sophia supplies Devin with feathers for his spells. He uses the softer and smaller feathers that come from her chest for spells involving peace or enlightenment. The wing feathers also prove useful for him, as with the following spell that I found particularly interesting:

"I will use her wing feathers in spells to help with creativity, especially in terms of the written arts," Devin explained. (You can see why this caught my interest.) "As a Pagan writer and journalist, this comes in handy often! A great spell for writer's block is to take a wing feather, dip it in ink, and then write 'writer's block' backward on a piece of parchment, then put the parchment in your Book of Shadows or on your altar. Works every time!"

Devin does not believe an animal, whether a bird or some other creature, can truly be a familiar if you do not treat it like one, and he has very definite ideas of how to go about this. "You have to spend time bonding with your familiar," he says. "Singing to it, chanting songs of power to it—or with it—and giving it its own name of power go a long way."

Any species of bird can be tamed as a familiar spirit, although what they have to offer in this context will vary considerably depending on the kind of bird you are working with. There is a world of difference between a macaw and a canary, not only in size but also in personality. What all birds require, though, is a commitment to their daily care. If the bird is to be a familiar, as Devin points out, it will also require additional time for bonding.

Our avian familiars will usually be caged house birds. A truly tame bird may not need to remain in its cage constantly—Sophia has her outings where she can stretch her wings—but for the most part they live in little homes that we keep in our much larger homes. In chapter 7 I will discuss keeping chickens as a means of participating more fully in the food cycle. If you decide to pursue this, your chickens could become familiars, assuming you spend a lot of your time outdoors with them. Usually, though, a bird kept as a familiar is a bird that lives indoors.

This chapter would be incomplete without mentioning reptiles and amphibians as familiars. Next to the cat, the most stereotypical familiar spirit might be the witch's toad. Herptiles (a collective word for both reptiles and amphibians) are often believed to be stupid, but it is perhaps more accurate to say that they have a very *alien* intelligence. As such, they can be fascinating familiars, opening our spirits to a very different world.

And that is all I am going to say about them.

Why? Because, quite honestly, most people have no business keeping herptiles in confinement. As I said, they have a very alien intelligence. Their minds and bodies are so different from our own. With a dog, a cat, a rabbit, or, to a lesser extent, even a bird, you can tell just by looking at the animal if it is distressed. Not so with herptiles. There is nothing at all intuitive about their care. Far too many reptiles and amphibians die in agony while in the care of well-meaning but uneducated humans.

If you must have a herptile as your familiar, I suggest the corn snake. These inoffensive creatures are easier to care for than most other cold-blooded creatures. But whatever reptile or amphibian you choose, learn everything you can about its needs before you purchase the animal. And don't trust the "expert advice" of a pet shop employee. Do some real research on your own. Prior to the 1970s, pet shops across the United States routinely sold pet turtles—red-eared sliders—along with cute plastic bowls to house them, and boxes of what was allegedly turtle food. What the shop employees failed to tell their customers was that the pets were newly hatched baby turtles that (if they lived) would grow to be up to a foot in length. The little turtle bowls were woefully inadequate, but this rarely mattered because the baby turtles had no idea that the brown junk sprinkled into their bowls was supposed to be "food," and almost all of them died miserably before the size of their housing actually became an issue.

If at all possible, talk to someone who breeds whatever reptile or amphibian you are interested in. Most herptiles will not readily reproduce if maintained under less than optimal conditions, so you can usually safely assume that a breeder understands the basic needs of the species in question. And do not think you can cut corners. If the breeder says the herptile requires a temperature range of 73 to 80 degrees, "room temperature" is not an acceptable alternative.

Almost any land-dwelling or amphibious species can be a familiar, and each has its own wisdom to offer us; each brings its own lessons to share. When we connect with familiars—with animal companions—we connect more deeply with the great web of life.

CHAPTER FIVE

LEAF AND FRUIT

In agricultural traditions like Plow Monday and wassailing fruit trees, rituals like the Anglo-Saxon Æcerbot charm to ensure the fertility of a field, or the women-only fertility rites of the Greek Thesmophoria, we see a common theme. It is apparent that the question originally addressed by Pagan religions was the same question that has been asked by every heterotrophic organism since the dawn of life.

What's for dinner?

This question is typically answered today with a trip to the supermarket or a local restaurant. We humans are less immediately involved with the source of our sustenance, and for the most part this is a good thing. Modern people living in any developed nation are not going to starve if there is a local drought or if a field of corn is ruined by insects or a fungus. For our Pagan ancestors, however, the question of what's for dinner was an ever-present concern. Whatever your cultural or biological heritage may be, most of your ancestors were directly involved with food acquisition: farming, hunting, or fishing.

They were directly dependent on the earth's bounty in a way that we can only imagine today. It was this continual dependence on the earth that gave rise to the earliest expressions of Pagan spirituality.

Everyone with an elementary understanding of Roman religion knows that Mars is a "war god." What is often overlooked is that Mars was originally a protector of the fields, a warrior who drove away the insect and fungal infestations that could ruin local crops. The oldest festival to Venus, the Roman goddess of love and beauty, was the Vinalia Rustica, when vegetable growth and fertility were celebrated. Likewise, the Norse god Thor is known as a god of thunder and storms (his Anglo-Saxon name, Thunor, is the Old English word for thunder), but it is less well known that he is also a god of fertility. The Greek god Dionysus is a god of wine, but he has an equally important role as the god who ensures the fertility and abundance of the grape harvest. The Gallo-Roman Epona, notable as a horse goddess, is also a goddess of fertility. A close examination of Pagan gods and goddesses reveals again and again how many of them have some association with the earth's bounty.

The simple act of growing some portion of your own food can help integrate your Pagan spirituality into a holistic lifestyle. I am not suggesting you buy a tractor and plow up the back forty. In the first place, it is highly improbable that you even have access to forty acres. And if you do, I would discourage you from taking on a project of that size! My recommendation to people who have done little gardening on their own is to start out on a very small scale. The most common mistake new gardeners make is to put in bigger gardens than they can maintain. The same vegetable garden that looked manageable in the early spring can become enormous by the middle of summer. The result is often an overgrown, weedy mess.

You do not need a lot of space to produce some healthy, homegrown food. Even if you only have the time and resources for a tiny, postage-stamp garden, you will be reclaiming a place in the eternal cycle of giving to and receiving from the earth.

How much space is required? Only as much as you can give, and as much as you have the time and enthusiasm to care for. Consider what can be produced on one square yard. In a temperate climate you can begin by planting spinach early in the spring. Spinach does best in cool weather and can be planted a couple of weeks before the last spring frost. If you plant your spinach seeds four inches apart, which is plenty of room for spinach, you can grow about eighty spinach plants on that square-yard plot of ground.

Harvest the spinach. It is early in the season, and your square-yard plot is ready for a new crop. So plant radishes this time. Radishes can be harvested in as little as three weeks after the seeds are planted. They can be spaced more closely than spinach, so plant your radish seeds three inches apart. With this spacing you can grow more than 140 radishes!

Harvest the radishes. It is now probably too late in the year for cool-weather crops like lettuce or spinach, but your square-yard plot is ready for seeds again. This time plant bush beans. Like spinach, bush bean seeds will have plenty of room to grow if you plant them four inches apart, giving you up to eighty bush bean plants on your square yard. I cannot tell you

exactly how many beans you will harvest, but the rough esti-
mate is "a lot."

After you have harvested your beans, it will be late enough
in the year, or close to it, for planting lettuce. (Or you could
plant lettuce in the spring and spinach in the autumn; the
point is that neither does very well in hot weather.) The best
varieties for a home garden are either bibb lettuce or leaf lettuce. Either can be planted about two months before the first
autumn frost is expected in your area. Lettuce seeds need to
be spaced six inches apart, but even given this generous spacing you can plant about thirty-five lettuce on your square yard.
Harvest this just before the first frost.

If you have been keeping track, you can see that one square
yard of earth can potentially yield eighty spinach plants, 140
radishes, a lot of bush beans on eighty plants, and thirty-five
lettuce plants. In one year.

To be fair, this is a very intensive usage of that square
yard plot. And you probably do not like at least one of the
four vegetables planted in my hypothetical tiny garden. (I
loathe radishes, which is a shame because they are one of
the easiest foods to grow.) You can see, though, how producing some of your own food does not demand an excessive
amount of space.

Does this sound tedious? If you have bought or are renting a home with even a small yard, you are *already* growing
things. These things are called "grass," perennial plants that
we cut down every week or two throughout the growing season. We humans have, in a way, become slaves to grass. We
feed the grass and water the grass, and carefully eliminate—
with our incessant mowing—the trees and shrubs that would

otherwise invade and compete with our grass overlords. And what does the grass give us in return? Not much.

It would take a lot of work to replace your entire lawn with a productive garden, and you probably would not be allowed to do so anyway. Cities and towns now usually have ordinances that require you to devote most of your front yard to a field of close-cut grass. (Yes, it seems that the grass overlords have even taken control of our government!) Even without these ordinances you probably would not want to do anything that drastic, nor would I encourage you to. Remember what I said about starting small!

Also, there is no need or reason to plan a garden as a square or rectangular plot in the middle of your back yard. My own vegetable garden borders my patio. This year two varieties of summer squash grow at each end of the patio border. Corn is coming up next to the holly bushes, which are the only purely "decorative" plants allowed. Between the corn and one of the varieties of squash are my potatoes. Three dozen tomato plants circle delightfully around the scarecrow we have standing just off the southwest corner of the patio.

Your garden can be attractive and pleasant as well as productive.

I also advise against planting in "rows." This is only beneficial if you are going to start up the tractor and cultivate large tracts of land. For a simple home garden, rows leave excessive gaps between plants. Any open space in your garden is space for weeds to invade and take over. Obviously you will need pathways allowing you to reach all of the plants, but these should be minimal.

CHARMING THE PLOW

All too often people's thoughts turn to gardening in the spring, when the forsythia and violets are in bloom and (in North America) the first robin is seen. Experienced gardeners begin planning and preparing long before then, and it has ever been so. The Anglo-Saxons gave "sol-cakes" as offerings to the Earth Mother in early February, but preparations for the growing season began even earlier than that. Even today, in England, the first Monday following Twelfth Day (January 6th) is known as Plow Monday. There were once traditional customs that varied from one region to another involving ceremonies in which plows were "charmed," or blessed. A plow was often decorated and processed through the village. The church abolished both the blessings and processions in the sixteenth century, but the tradition of the plow procession was later revived in some areas (Simpson and Roud, p. 281).

While charming the plow may seem like little more than a quaint custom, it can have very practical consequences. Few of us today have a plow that we will hitch up to a draft horse or a pair of oxen, but we do have gardening tools. Every year I participate in a charming rite, but for my own group this is a more contemporary "charming of the rotary tiller." If your garden is too small to bother with a rotary tiller, not to worry; any gardening tool can be charmed: hoes, shovels, forks, trowels. The practical consequence comes into play when you gather up these tools and really look at them for the first time since you put them away the previous autumn. If the shovel's blade is bent, you will have time to repair or replace it before you really need a shovel. If the handle on your tiller is loose, you can tighten it now. Your gardening tools will be cleaned up and ready to use in preparation for the growing season.

A charming ritual also honors the spirits within the participants' tillers and other gardening tools. Some readers may find it strange to think of non-living things as having spirits, but people who work with the spirit realm very often report interactions with these entities. The Findhorn Garden was established in the 1960s by an intentional community in Scotland. Members of this community nurtured lush and productive gardens with the guidance they received from entities they referred to as "devas." Most of these were the spirits of living things—a spinach deva, a pear deva, a tomato deva, and so on—but the Findhorn community was also contacted by a machine deva informing them that machines and tools respond to love and care just as living things do (Findhorn Community, p. 162).

Contemporary Pagans, in the United States at least, who hold charming the plow rituals most often do these near the end of January or in early February near the holy tide known variously as Candlemas, Imbolc, Ewemeolc, and by other names. If you are developing Hal Sidu—evolving your own holistic traditions—the time to bless your gardening tools should be appropriate to your local environment. Plow Monday falls in January because England, warmed by the Gulf Stream, has a relatively mild climate. The soil can be tilled there earlier than in many temperate regions. Your own charming ritual should take place about a month or so before you intend to begin gardening.

When I lived in Missouri, my ritual of charming the rotary tiller took place in early February because I began preparing my garden in March and then would begin planting in April. Then I moved to western Pennsylvania. Although the summers and winters are both milder there than the severe seasons experienced in the heartland, Pennsylvania has a significantly shorter growing season. After putting in my first garden, I watched my tomato plants as they suffered under three heavy snowfalls. (Amazingly, some of the plants survived.) I knew the seasons and cycles of the earth in Missouri, but I was ignorant of Pennsylvania's natural cycles. My spiritual traditions were not aligned with the forces around me.

Now, knowing that Pennsylvania can have snow as late as May, I hold my charming ritual at or near the spring equinox. I could still do it in early February, but the ritual would lose much of its significance. Your own ritual should likewise be held a month or so before you will begin working with the earth. Charming the plow prepares us mentally for the coming year even as we organize our gardening implements.

For your charming the plow ritual, all you will need is a pleasing essential oil and, naturally, whatever gardening tools you intend to bless. This can be included as part of another ritual if that works for you. The first thing you need to do, before the ritual begins, is cleanse each gardening tool. Literally. Wash off any dirt, and, while doing this, see if any part of the implement has broken or become loose. You may want to decorate the tool with a bit of ribbon. After this, small trowels and similar implements can be placed on the altar, while shovels, hoes, and (if you use one) a rotary tiller can be placed near the altar and to one side.

When you are ready for the charming, anoint each gardening implement with your essential oil as you address it, saying:

Hail to you and to the spirit within you!
May you greet the Earth, Mother of All Life.
Let her be full of growth and abundant with nourishment.

Finish with a final expression of affirmation. I would say, "Ic bidde thé nu" (eech bidda they noo), which means "I ask you now" in Old English. Your own affirmation should be an appropriate expression of your spirituality. Wiccans, for example, might say, "So mote it be."

Having blessed, or charmed, your gardening tools, keep them in a clean, dry place until you are ready to prepare your garden.

BIDDING THE LAND

Here we are using the word *bid* in the sense of praying or entreating, a meaning that comes from the Old English verb *biddan*. If you are planting a garden to help integrate your spirituality with your daily activities, your first step is to entreat the land itself and develop a positive relationship with the spirit beings that reside in that vicinity. This is important even if you are taking over someone else's vegetable garden or converting a former flower garden. The land is not just a thing; it has a life of its own.

You will need either cornmeal or oatmeal (real oatmeal, not the processed instant stuff), enough to scoop up five handfuls. You will also need a spade or shovel. Decide where and how large your garden will be. If this is your first garden, I recommend that you limit the size to no more than one hundred square feet. This can be a ten-foot square, a five-foot-by-twenty-foot rectangle, or any other shape you can imagine. Of course it can be much smaller if you prefer. What matters is that it not be too large. Your garden should continue to be a source of pride and pleasure throughout the growing season, and this will not happen if it is too large to easily maintain.

Go to the eastern edge of the garden. Use your spade or shovel to dig a small hole. It need not be more than a few inches deep. Facing the east, sprinkle a handful of meal into this hole as you say:

> *Eastward I stand,*
> *for favors I pray.*
> *I ask the spirits who dance in this place,*
> *I ask the ancestors who watch over this place,*
> *I ask of Mother Earth and Father Sky,*
> *accept now this offering of grain,*
> *and ever there be peace between us.*

Fill in the hole with soil as you express a final affirmation, just as you did in the charming the plow rite in the previous section.

Now go to the southern edge of the garden and dig a second hole there. Facing south, sprinkle a handful of meal into the hole and say the same prayer, substituting "Southward stand I" for "Eastward stand I." Fill this hole with soil, speaking your affirmation, as you did with the eastern hole.

Repeat this again at the western edge of the garden and then again at the northern edge. If your garden has an irregular shape, these four holes may not be equidistant from each other, but that does not matter.

Go to the very center of the garden—or to what seems like the center if your garden has an irregular shape—and dig a fifth hole. Sprinkle one last handful of meal into this hole as you say:

> *Holy Mother Earth,*
> *May the you and the spirits herein*
> *let this land grow and thrive,*
> *increase and strengthen,*
> *with tall stems and fine crops.*
> *May this sacred land be protected from harm*
> *and warded against all ills.*

Fill in this last hole as you speak your words of affirmation. Having given your offerings of meal, the rite is now complete.

The wording and procedure of this rite are only suggestions. If your spirituality demands a different approach to bidding the land, by all means be true to your gods and your chosen path! I confess that the rite I have given has an Anglo-Saxon bias. The wording of the prayers is borrowed and modified from the eleventh-century Æcerbot, or "land ceremonies charm" (Griffiths, pp. 173–75). These prayers had been heavily Christianized by the time the charm was written down—with numerous references to saints, the Lord's

Prayer, crucifixes, and so on—but the Earth Mother was still addressed as a living, sentient entity.

Since your garden is intended to strengthen your connection with the earth and attune you to nature's cycles, plan your gardening activities "by the moon." This involves two different factors. The first (and, in my opinion, the most important) of these is the moon's phase: whether the moon is growing larger or smaller, and which phase of the cycle it is in. Everyone who gardens by the moon plans his or her activities according to the moon's phase. The second factor is which sign of the zodiac the moon is in on any given day. Like the sun and the planets, the moon travels through all twelve signs of the zodiac, twelve equal divisions of the sky named after constellations of the classical world. But while it takes the sun about a month to move through a sign of the zodiac, the moon moves from one sign to the next every two or three days.

Determining the moon's phase is very easy; just look up in the sky at night! If you have not been paying attention previous to this, it may take two or three months to be sure exactly where the moon is in its cycle. The general rules for planting by the moon's phase are equally easy:

- When the moon is *waxing* (growing larger, from new to full), plant vegetables and fruits that bear above ground. This includes most of what you will probably be growing.
- When the moon is *waning* (growing smaller, from full to new), plant vegetables that bear below ground: potatoes, carrots, radishes, and so on. Ideally these should be planted while the moon is still in its *third quarter* (growing smaller, but still half full or larger).

• When the moon is in its *fourth quarter* (growing small-er, and less than half full), weed the garden and destroy pests.

If you want to include the moon's zodiac sign in your garden planning, you will need a current almanac. *The Old Farmer's Almanac* is sold in bookstores, drugstores, and super-markets across the United States. This annual publication always includes the moon's astrological position throughout the year, as well as a page or more of advice about planting and doing other activities by the moon. Although not as widely available, an even better resource is *Llewellyn's Moon Sign Book*. I prefer this publication because it gives the time of day that the moon changes from one sign to the next, which the for-mer publication lacks. Llewellyn's guide is filled with interest-ing information about the moon and astrological influences.

The general rules for planting by the moon's signs are:

• Plant seeds or transplant young plants when the moon is in either a water sign (Cancer, Scorpio, Pisces) or an earth sign (Taurus, Virgo, Capricorn).

• Weed and control pests when the moon is in either a fire sign (Aries, Leo, Sagittarius) or an air sign other than Libra (Gemini, Aquarius).

• Plant flowers when the moon is in Libra.

As you can see, an ideal time to plant most vegetable seeds would be when the moon is waxing and in the sign of either Cancer, Scorpio, or Pisces. In the real world, for people who hold regular jobs and juggle their free time between family, housecleaning, and other obligations, the "ideal time" may not come at a reasonable time. When this happens, find the best compromise available. When circumstances prevent you from planting while the moon is in an earth or water sign, just be sure to do it while the moon is waxing (or in its third quarter if you are planting potatoes or carrots). If instead you cannot plant during the best phase of the moon, plant when the moon is in the right zodiac sign.

You may decide that you would like to grow herbs instead of vegetables. This may be especially appealing if you have limited space for your garden. Although a small plot can yield a substantial quantity of vegetables, it will not produce more than a miniscule portion of the food you and your family will consume. However that same small plot, with careful planning, could easily supply you with several varieties of culinary herbs, and that may be more satisfying for you.

Of course herbs have many uses, and there is no reason why you could not plant a garden of remedial (medicinal) herbs or cosmetic herbs. You could even plant aromatic herbs for making your own incense and potpourri, which we will discuss in a later chapter. The reason I emphasize culinary herbs here is because of the adage "You are what you eat." By planting herbs, vegetables, or fruits that you will later eat, you will participate more completely in that eternal cycle of taking and giving back to the earth, the cycle that gave rise to humankind's earliest and most persistent Pagan rites.

There are no defining boundaries between remedial, culinary, or cosmetic herbs other than the uses we put them to. Some of your culinary herbs will have remedial uses, and some will have cosmetic or aromatic uses, but some may have no purpose other than to taste good when added to recipes. If you have the space and inclination, you could grow both vegetables and herbs in your garden.

FRIGE'S GARDEN

In the fifth century, in Europe, Mary was proclaimed to be the mother of God, and in the years that followed, "Mary's gardens" became popular features both in monasteries and on private estates. These gardens were planted with flowers and herbs. They provided a private place for prayer and contemplation. The Mary's garden was usually a very small garden, especially in overcrowded medieval towns and cities. Most featured a small statue of the Virgin Mary as a focal point of the garden.

The Mary's garden is a Christian tradition, but you can create a similar garden dedicated to a goddess from your pantheon as an expression of your own Pagan spirituality. This works especially well if you prefer to grow herbs rather than vegetables. Since a garden of this kind is intended for contemplation and prayer, a variety of attractive and aromatic herbs will create the appropriate ambiance.

For a Saxon Pagan, this would most likely be a Frige's garden, dedicated to Woden's consort. Frige gave her name to the sixth day of the week, Friday (Frigesdæg). She is sovereign over marriages, families, and household arts. In a modern context, Frige is also sovereign over business enterprises, because "household arts," for the Anglo-Saxons, included cloth making, soap making, dyeing, medicine, weaving, and pretty much any occupation other than hunting, fishing, and warfare.

A Frige's garden can be planted with rosemary, sage, chamomile, fennel, alecost, and feverfew. All of these herbs were known to the Anglo-Saxons, either because they are indigenous to England or because they were brought there by the Romans. Adding a few marigolds to the garden will add decorative color and will discourage rabbits that might otherwise be tempted to munch on your herbs. Outdoor statues of Frige are not readily available, but there are other ways to represent the goddess. Some people believe the goose is sacred to Frige. I know of no historical mention of this, but the goose is a monogamous bird, which is appropriate for any animal that would be sacred to a goddess of marriage. If you cannot find or do not care for a statue of a goose, find a large stone and engrave or paint Frige's name on it using Anglo-Saxon runes:

ᚠᚱᛁᚷᛖ

A seat or small bench will provide a restful place to enjoy the garden and commune with Frige.

If you follow a different spiritual path, you will of course want to dedicate your garden to another goddess. Every Pagan pantheon has at least a couple goddesses who could be honored in a garden such as this.

The Roman Pagan can create a Juno's garden using Roman herbs such as basil, catnip, dill, oregano, rue, and wormwood. The Juno's garden might include a small bay laurel tree, which in cooler climates would need to be brought inside in the autumn. Terracotta pots can be used to create a Mediterranean atmosphere.

Hellenic Pagans can dedicate Hera's gardens or Aphrodite's gardens and plant them with wild celery, borage, elecampane, thyme, calendula, and horehound. Statues of Greek or Roman goddesses can sometimes be found in garden shops. A basic Doric column is another statuary design that would enhance a garden dedicated to any Greek goddess.

A Brigid's garden would be appropriate for an Irish Pagan. This garden could be planted with yarrow, vervain, self-heal, and comfrey. Include either some white or red clover, both of which are considered shamrocks by the Irish. Avoid the large-leafed "lucky shamrocks" sold around St. Patrick's Day. Despite their visual appeal, these are actually tropical plants native to South America.

Whichever goddess you honor in your garden, be sure to also plant a selection of culinary herbs—herbs that you will later consume—to ensure that you share in the cycle of taking and giving back.

BALCONY GARDENS

But what if you have no land at all? How can the apartment dweller connect with the food cycle?

Connecting with the earth is obviously going to be more challenging under these circumstances, but the problem is not insurmountable. An apartment balcony can be transformed into a small garden for either herbs or vegetables. Plants such as comfrey or potatoes that have a deep or extensive root system do not work well in balcony gardens, but many herbs and vegetables can thrive just outside your third-story apartment.

Lettuce and radishes both grow easily in just a few inches of soil. A five-gallon pickle barrel, with drainage holes

drilled or punched in the bottom, can support a cherry tomato plant. You can even purchase large pots designed specifically for growing strawberries! Most culinary herbs can be
grown in balcony pots.

You will have to work harder to maintain a balcony garden because Mother Earth is not there to help you. Potted
plants are more susceptible to temperature changes and
drought. You will need to check your plants at least every
other day to make sure their soil is not too dry, and perennial herbs (plants that live for more than two years) usually will
not survive the winter outside in pots.

There is no point in bidding the land when creating a balcony garden since you are not working directly with the land
itself. Nevertheless, remember that the soil you have carried
up to your balcony in bags or buckets came from the body of
Mother Earth. After you have filled your pots or other growing containers with soil, burn some incense and say:

> *I ask the spirits who dance in this place,*
> *I ask the ancestors who watch over this place,*
> *I ask of Mother Earth and Father Sky,*
> *accept now this offering of sweet incense,*
> *and ever there be peace between us.*

If you do not have a yard or balcony, try a windowsill garden. This will be even more challenging, but there are some
culinary herbs that will grow indoors. Chives and basil both
work well.

Chives, in fact, work best as a potted plant. Even if you
have three acres at your disposal, consider keeping a pot of

chives on your patio or inside near a sunny window. Whenever you are serving dinner with a dish that can be enhanced with fresh chives—such as steak or baked potatoes—set your pot of chives in the center of the table as you would a flower arrangement, and place a clean pair of kitchen shears next to the pot. Invite your family members or guests to clip their own fresh chives right off the plant!

Whether your garden is large or tiny, whether you want to grow mostly vegetables or mostly herbs, only plant what you will actually use. I once planted a lot of rue in my herb garden because it sounded magical and intriguing. The rue grew very well, but I had no idea what to do with it. This does not mean that rue has no useful purpose. I have a friend who is a Roman Pagan, and she uses rue all the time. But it is not something I use. As a result, my garden rue was very pretty, but it took up garden space where I could have planted something more practical.

That should have been the end of the story, but I am a slow learner. Several years later I planted radishes in my vegetable garden because I had heard they are easy to grow and can be harvested in just a few weeks. And, yes, they grew abundantly. As promised, within a few weeks I had a bumper crop of radishes—a bumper crop of something I cannot stand the taste of. (I even pick out the little radish slivers they inevitably put into salads at restaurants.) Fortunately, the radishes only took up space in my garden for a few weeks, but they were weeks when I could have been growing something that I actually like to eat.

To grow a successful garden, then, your first priority is to plant things that you will happily consume. The purpose of the garden, after all, is to help you connect with the earth by producing some small portion of your own food.

INTENTIONAL PLANTING

Thus far our focus has been on plants that produce food, and for good reason. Most Pagans describe our many paths as "earth-focused" spirituality and agree that Paganism implies a love for the earth. But how can we claim to love or even understand the earth's rhythms if we never *touch* the earth? How can we claim any connection with the land when every bite of our food is shipped to us from distant places? Through gardening we gain an appreciation for what "fertility" meant to our ancestors. Furthermore, we literally become a part of the land itself. As we work the soil, our skin cells slough away, falling to the earth and becoming part of it. We nurture the land, and food comes forth, and the land becomes a part of us as we take that food into our bodies.

If you find that you really enjoy gardening, you can take it even further and plant herbs and shrubs to benefit the wild folk who live around you. Pagan people with holistic traditions live in the world, not apart from it. Our neighbors are not only the humans who live to either side of us; they include the mammals, birds, reptiles, amphibians, arthropods, and other life forms in our immediate vicinity. Like every creature, we humans must sometimes protect our territory, but, as a whole, Pagans usually want to live peacefully with the furred, feathered, and scaled children of Mother Earth. We can help our non-human neighbors by creating beneficial habitats for them.

These habitats are for living, incarnate creatures, but I believe this is also pleasing to the nature spirits. As a Saxon, I call these spirits "elves," but other cultures have given them other names. The elves (or whatever you choose to call them) nurture the natural world around us, and so it makes sense that they would be happy with any effort we make to help create a healthy and diverse environment.

Honeybees are kept everywhere by amateur and professional beekeepers. A hive produces both honey and beeswax. Honeybees also play an important role in pollinating fruit trees. The most difficult time of the year for honeybees is early spring, when the hive's supply of pollen and honey is depleted. Beekeepers help out their little friends by feeding them sugar water, but you can do your part, too. Pussy willows and redbud trees are attractive, and both are excellent sources of pollen and nectar in the early spring. Later in the year, white clover provides nectar. White clover can be seeded directly into your lawn, and benefits the grasses already growing there by fixing nitrogen into the soil. Very few plants provide enough nectar for bees to produce excess honey for our use. In any given vicinity, there will only be one or two plants that produce that much nectar. Clover is one of those plants. The honeybees collect nectar from white and yellow clovers. It is difficult for them to gather nectar from the blossoms of red clover, but this variety is very beneficial to bumblebees. Even if you live in a region that produces a non-clover honey (buckwheat, mesquite, and so on), your white clover will benefit local hives.

If you grow a variety of herbs, some of them will provide nectar for local honeybees and enjoy visits from these little insects throughout the summer. Honeybees are especially attracted to sage, but they will also gather nectar from marjoram, winter savory, lemon balm, thyme, mint, and other herbs.

Intentional planting can also provide food sources for birds. You can hang out a bird feeder—and I do—but ideally this only supplements foods that the birds can gather from natural sources. One of the best shrubs for winter feeding is the pyrocantha, or fire thorn bush. This bush produces scarlet or orange-red berries, depending on the species, which apparently do not taste very good to birds. For this reason, pyrocantha berries are available to the birds that remain with us all winter long after other natural foods have been eaten. Holly also serves the same purpose. If holly grows well in your area, there is an additional benefit: you can cut and bring boughs of it inside the house to deck your Yuletide halls!

Other good shrubs that provide food for winter birds include barberry, privet, and coralberry.

When spring arrives, many birds will eat the blossoms of forsythia, lilac, and honeysuckle. But at this point, the birds have a need other than food. They need housing; specifically, nesting sites. The housing conditions for birds fall into three general categories: ground nests, cavity nests, and tree nests. We cannot intentionally prepare a place for ground-nesting birds, and the cavity-nesting birds are best served with birdhouses. My grandfather provided housing for a diverse variety of birds by setting out different houses for purple martins, wrens, titmice, and chickadees.

Tree-nesting birds require trees and shrubs for building their nests. No single tree or shrub will satisfy the needs of all tree-nesting species. Some of these birds will only build nests at the ends of tree branches. Others build their nests in the "V" of two limbs. Still others hide their nests deep within thick shrubs. The best way to provide nesting sites for these species is to give them as wide a variety of woody growth—trees and shrubs—as you reasonably can. Some of the best trees for tree-nesting birds are apples, hawthorns, maples, oaks, pines, and willows. For bushes, good choices include blackberry, juniper, pyrocantha, and raspberry.

All wild creatures, regardless of species or phylum, share one common need. Whether honeybee or gray squirrel, goldfinch or garter snake, every living thing must have water to survive. The easiest way to offer water to your wild neighbors is by setting out a birdbath. Despite the name, the "bath" provides water for drinking as much as or more than for bathing. And it is usable by more than just birds; in dry weather, some insects—including honeybees—will take water from a birdbath.

If you are more ambitious, a small pond will supply water to a greater range of wildlife. The pond need not be more than a few feet in diameter. It should be deep enough to leave some water beneath the ice during the coldest days of winter. At one time, building a small pond was a significant undertaking, but today you can purchase pond liners at your local garden shop. All you need to do is dig a hole, put in the liner, and fill the thing with water. You can add decorative rocks around the border or put in an ornamental fountain, but that is just icing on the cake.

Put a few inexpensive "feeder" goldfish in the pond to eliminate any problem with mosquitoes, but let the water set for a few days first. Tap water is treated with chlorine, which will kill your fish if you put them in just after filling the pond.

Ponds such as these are often called "lily ponds," and it really is a good idea to put in one or more lily plants. The leaves will float on the surface, helping to stabilize the temperature of the water while simultaneously discouraging the growth of excessive algae and providing some protection from predators.

This is why you want the pond deep enough so the water will not freeze all the way to the bottom. If you aren't sure how deep your pond needs to be, check with your local pet or garden supply house. You can leave the fish and lily bulbs in the pond throughout the year. The water at the bottom of the pond may get very cold, but the fish and lily plants will survive. In addition, you may attract a few new wild neighbors that you were not expecting—frogs! My own pond has become home to some leopard frogs, which I consider a blessing. There is something very magical about frogs, living in a liminal place between the land and the water. In folklore, the magic of frogs is the magic of transformation. This undoubtedly comes from their change from aquatic tadpoles to amphibious air breathers, and has inspired folk tales such as the story of the Frog Prince.

Throughout this book I have made the assumption that most readers are Pagan people living in urban or suburban environments with limited space. You may be the exception, with a large expanse of property to call your own. If so, consider setting some of your land aside as sacred space for your gods and the local nature spirits. We humans are so quick to grab up every bit of available space, cutting across natural territories with our roads and highways and clearing out habitats to make way for more strip malls. What greater act of devotion can there be than to give over some part of your land to the wild?

But to do this with any real meaning, you have to be sincere. If you give some land to your gods and the nature spirits, then it is no longer yours to use; it's theirs. This can be a difficult idea for some people to embrace. We tend to presume eminent domain over all the earth.

A third of "my" property has been set aside for the elves. When I mentioned this to a group of Pagans, one man immediately responded enthusiastically, saying, "We should hold a ritual there some day!" It took some time to explain to him that the land is not mine—except within the context of human law—and so we would be trespassing.

Back there, on that sacred land I have set aside, oaks and ivy grow undisturbed. Small mammals scurry about without fear of human interference. Birds nest in the trees and shrubs. That is the outer realm, and it is not mine to use. It is the home of elves, hobs, and moss-wives. It is within my inner realm that I grow corn, squash, pumpkins, and tomatoes; where frogs greet me in the morning and red-breasted robins search for bugs in the garden.

When we really touch the earth, our Pagan spirituality comes alive.

CHAPTER SIX

BARK AND BRANCH

In the last chapter we mentioned trees as nesting sites for some birds, but trees are much more than habitats for wildlife. Whether due to their longevity or size, trees are often accorded a status higher than other botanical species. "Save a tree" is the environmental battle cry. You are unlikely to hear anyone saying "save a dandelion," even though dandelions provide food for honeybees, discourage army worms, and help break up hardened soil. Dandelions and most other plants just do not command the same degree of respect that we have for trees.

Admittedly, it takes longer to replace a tree than a dandelion, but our arboreal veneration arises from a deeper, spiritual association we have with trees that is often reflected in Pagan myths and folklore. From a Saxon perspective, every wooded grove is the domain of the *wudu-elfen*, the spirits who nurture and sustain forest ecology. Larger woodlands are home to satyr-like spirit beings known as *woodwoses*. To senselessly pollute or destroy these wild places is no less an offense than vandalizing a neighbor's house. The trees themselves, for the Saxon Pagan, embody sacred mysteries. No less than five of these trees—the oak, ash, hawthorn, yew, and birch—are described in the Old English Rune Poem, a tenth-century document recording the mystic lore associated with twenty-nine runic symbols known as the Futhorc (Albertsson, *Wyrdworking*, pp. 89–107).

The Saxons' veneration of trees was passed from one generation to the next, long after Christianity became the dominant religion in England. Perhaps the most revered of trees is the oak. Simpson and Roud say that the oak tree represents "steadfast courage, royalty and England" (p. 264). In Pagan times, the oak was sacred to Thunor, a god of thunder and fertility. For this reason it was commonly believed (although this is not true) that oak trees can never be struck by lightning.

The restoration of the English monarchy is celebrated on May 29th, which is known as Royal Oak Day. King Charles II is said to have hidden in the hollow of an oak tree, thus evading capture during the Battle of Worcester. After his return to London in 1660, it became a custom to wear an oak leaf every May 29th. The original oak that sheltered King Charles is now gone, but a descendant called "Son of Oak" still stands in Boscobel Wood.

Son of Oak is the tree most associated with Charles's escape during the English Civil War, but other trees along the route of his exodus are also said to have hidden him from the Roundheads: an oak tree in Gloucestershire, an elm in Sussex. Charles II seems to have had a very good relationship with the wood spirits!

The Parliament Oak in Nottinghamshire is so called because King John (or King Edward, depending on whom you ask) is said to have convened a Parliament there.

The grandest of England's notable oaks must surely be the Major Oak, in Sherwood Forest. According to legend, this tree is where Robin Hood convened his Merry Men. The Major Oak is certainly old enough for this distinction. Having stood for more than a thousand years, it now has a trunk circumference of thirty-five feet. The Major Oak's heavier limbs are held in place by wooden poles installed by dedicated caretakers to ensure that the limbs do not collapse under their own weight.

The hawthorn, in England, is a tree with a mixed reputation. Bringing hawthorn blossoms into the house supposedly invites ill fortune. On the other hand, the Holy Thorn of Glastonbury was considered a sacred tree. It was believed that the tree had grown from a single thorn taken from Christ's "crown of thorns." You would think that would have negative connotations rather than positive; and apparently the Puritans thought the whole story was evil, because a Roundhead (one of the Puritan rebels who opposed the monarchy) eventually destroyed the tree. However, by that time many cuttings had been taken from the Glastonbury Thorn, and its descendants are held in respect to this day.

In some parts of England, the hawthorn was believed to have protective powers. Hawthorn branches were traditionally burned in Herefordshire on New Year's Day to protect the future crop from evil spirits as well as from a disease known as "smut."

The rowan, or mountain ash, was credited as a protection against negative magic. In Yorkshire, rowan twigs were hung over doors and beds, and replaced with fresh twigs every year to replenish the protection. In Lancashire, rowan twigs were hung over beds specifically to repel the mare (MAR-eh), a malicious spirit that attacks a person while he or she is sleeping. In some places, the staff of a butter churn was made of rowan to ward against spells intended to spoil the butter.

Specific to Germanic cultures is the belief in multiple planes of existence connected through the roots and branches of a vast World Tree that was known to the Norse as Yggdrasil. This World Tree was often described as an ash tree, but occasionally as an elm. Its roots descended down to the realm of the dead, while its highest branches touched the celestial world of the gods.

The Maypole is most likely a representation of the World Tree. The pole is often said to be a phallic symbol, but I think this is a post-Freudian belief. The traditional European Maypole often displayed symbols of a village's trades on side "branches," and would be ceremoniously decorated at the top with garlands and a leafy tree branch (Jones and Pennick, p. 113). None of these adornments suggest a phallus, but they do suggest the image of a great tree. The trade symbols and garlands would interfere with the plaited ribbons we associate with modern Maypole dances, but ribbons did not come into use with Maypole dancing until the 1830s (Simpson and Roud, p. 230). Before then—and in some parts of Europe today—people either joined hands as they danced around the Maypole or danced solo.

Tree veneration is not unique to northern Europe. The Greeks told a tale of the goddess Athena and the god Poseidon having an argument about the possession of Attica. Both deities wanted to be sovereign over the region. To settle the issue, they each produced a gift and asked a mortal king, Cecrops, to judge which of the gifts was most worthy. Poseidon struck a rock with his trident, and a saltwater spring appeared. (Or a horse, depending on which version of the story you hear. I think the horse makes more sense. Of what use is a saltwater spring?) Clever Athena created an olive tree. King Cecrops judged the olive tree to be the more worthy gift, and so Athena became the patron of Attica.

From a Hellenic perspective, forests and woodlands are the home of dryads, or wood nymphs. The woodlands are also home to the satyr, a wild spirit similar to the Anglo-Saxon woodwose.

The Religio Romana, the religion of Pagan Rome, has a god named Silvanus who presides specifically over forests and trees. This forest god is a patron not only of wild woodlands, but of all arboriculture, including orchards.

Kemetic (Egyptian) Pagans are familiar with the story of the god Set murdering his brother Osiris. Set tricked Osiris into lying down inside a chest. Set and his accomplices then nailed the chest shut and threw it into the Nile. The chest floated down the river and out to sea until it eventually reached Phoenicia. There it rested against a tamarisk tree, which grew rapidly and enclosed the entire chest until the goddess Isis (Osiris's wife) later claimed her husband's corpse.

Slavic Pagans have the Leshy, a green-bearded spirit of the woodlands who stands as tall as the tallest trees in the depths of a forest, but becomes a tiny creature at the forest's edge. The Leshy is a mischievous spirit who often leads mortals astray if they venture too far into a forest, though he is generally considered to be good-natured.

Forest gods and woodland spirits are common to many Pagan paths. There are different ways a contemporary Pagan can integrate this into his or her spiritual practice. In all probability you already do! Many Pagans today set up and decorate evergreen trees at the winter solstice. You may even have heard that this is an ancient Pagan tradition that was later stolen by the Christians, but this is not true. In 575 CE, a Portuguese bishop complained about the Pagan custom of bringing "laurel and green branches" inside at Christmas, but people did not carry entire trees into their homes until the fifteenth century, and then only in Germany. Another four hundred years would pass before the custom started to become popular in other nations.

This does not make the tradition of the modern Yule tree any less valid. Every tradition—whether five years old, five hundred years old, or five thousand years old—had to begin sometime! The Yule tree is a beautiful custom for Pagan families, and we will look at this in more depth in this book's final chapter.

THE MIDSUMMER TREE

Why not take this tree veneration further, and add a Midsummer tree to your summer solstice celebration? One reason so many Pagans love the Yule season is because they associate

it with joyful activities. A holistic Pagan lifestyle should celebrate each holiday in a similar way, but all too often Midsummer or the equinoxes are acknowledged with little more than
an obligatory ritual.

Children love decorating a Midsummer tree, but it is fun
for adults as well. Midsummer, the summer solstice, is opposite the Yule season, so it makes sense to decorate a Midsummer tree that is opposite to the Yule tree.

This means you will be decorating a tree outside rather
than bringing a tree into the house. It also means that you
will be decorating a deciduous tree (one that drops its leaves
in the autumn) rather than an evergreen. If you live in a
warm climate where trees do not drop their leaves seasonally, just pick a tree that is pleasing to you. There is no actual
rule about leaf dropping, but it is important that the tree be
growing naturally outdoors. This changes the general ambiance of the tree veneration. When the Yule tree is brought
indoors, we are celebrating home and community. We may
derive a much deeper meaning from this, but essentially we
are gathering "at the hearth." The Midsummer tree, by contrast, is a celebration of the natural world, of the greater
place that surrounds our homes.

Choose a day near the summer solstice for decorating your
Midsummer tree. If your whole family is to participate, this
will probably need to be on a weekend. Also choose a tree that
will receive this honor. The honored tree needs to be a tree
with low-growing limbs. You will also need some or all of the
following:

- Dry pine cones
- Peanut butter

- Millet, or a mix of "bird seed"

- Assorted fruits

- String

- Scissors

- Several knives

The Midsummer tree is a celebration of the natural world, so you do not want to cover it with glass and plastic ornaments! You will be making your own ornaments, and not only will these be natural, they will be your offerings to the wudu-elfen or the dryads, or to Silvanus or the Leshy, or to whatever gods or entities your spiritual path associates with the woodlands.

Small children will require supervision with knives and scissors, but otherwise let your imagination run free! Each ornament should be made with the intention of supporting and sustaining the wild neighbors—the birds and mammals and butterflies—that live around us. (Some municipalities discourage leaving food out for wildlife due to a concern about rats and other vermin. Be sure you are not breaking any local ordinances.)

Cut an apple, orange, or other fruit into wedges and run a string through each wedge to hang it from a tree branch. You have your first ornaments!

Using the flat side of a knife, press peanut butter into the gaps in a pine cone. Then roll the pine cone in millet (or bird seed), pressing it down so that the seeds adhere to the peanut butter. Put a string through this, and you have a completely different ornament.

If you do not have any pine cones, cut an apple, pear, or similar solid fruit into wedges. "Paint" one side of a wedge with peanut butter, then press this into a bowl of millet. Add the string, and you have yet another ornament.

Use your imagination. You may decide to pop some corn and string it in garlands, or to string grapes or ripened berries. Part of the fun of the Midsummer tree is coming up with new and creative offerings to hang from the tree.

After you have a good assortment of natural ornaments, process outside to your chosen tree. At this point, how you honor the tree with your ornaments should reflect your own spiritual path, and can be as simple or as elaborate as you like. After hanging the fruits and cones from the tree limbs, you might conclude with a short prayer. Your prayer could be something like this:

Good neighbors,
you spirits of the land and air and water,
accept these gifts,
and may we ever meet and live together in peace.

There may be a much longer prayer that you find more appropriate. Or maybe you would rather have a more celebratory tradition, singing as you hang the offerings from the tree. On the other hand, if you live within earshot of your neighbors, they might think you are a bit odd when they hear you singing to the maple tree in your back yard.

On the other hand, maybe you do not care.

The Midsummer tree can evolve into a beautiful tradition for you and your family if you do this every year. I remember

returning to a hickory tree on the day after the summer solstice, when we had earlier decorated it with natural ornaments.
A finch flew away, startled by my arrival, and butterflies hov-
ered over the orange and red fruits that hung from the branches. The tree looked beautiful, and it seemed to me that the
wood elves were quite happy with our gifts.

After (or before) your coven or kindred decorates the Midsummer tree, you can extend the celebration by identifying
the different trees growing around your neighborhood. Many
people today cannot distinguish between a hickory and an ash,
but this is primarily because they have never bothered to really look at the botanical beings that live around them. Obtain a
tree identification guide from your bookstore or library, and
get everyone involved! If there are children in your tribe, let
them gather leaves and paste them into scrapbooks along with
the name of the tree that each leaf came from.

THE URBAN ORCHARD

If you have your own land, your tree veneration can include
some arboriculture that will complement your garden. You
can plant a few "decorative" trees around the outside of your
home, but keep in mind that *all* trees are decorative! Why
not plant trees that will increase your participation in the natural cycle by producing delicious fruits or nuts? Few trees are
more beautiful than a pear when it blossoms in early spring.

An orchard is any area of land devoted to the cultivation
of trees that bear edible fruits or nuts. It does not need to
have the regimented look of a rural fruit orchard, nor does it
need to feature only one kind of tree. In fact, your neighbors
are unlikely to notice an orchard at all when they see your

plum tree growing at the corner of your house, the pear tree in the back yard, and the Chinese chestnut on the north side of your garage.

The disadvantage of growing your own fruit and nut trees is that it will take at least a couple years before you see any produce, and usually longer. The advantage is that once the trees start producing, they keep producing! As you watch your fruit trees drop their leaves in the autumn and bear tiny new leaves in the spring, followed by beautiful blossoms and then heavy, ripe fruit, you will come to a deeper inner appreciation of the eternal cycle of life. Then, as with the vegetables you grow, you will take that fruit into your own body and literally become one with the land around you.

Many fruit trees are now sold in standard, dwarf, and even miniature versions. For the urban orchard, dwarf trees are often the best choice. You will be able to reach more of the fruit since the tree will not grow as tall, and it will not take up as much space on your property. If you have an especially small lot, consider a miniature fruit tree.

Since both fruit trees and nut trees produce their bounty above ground, you will want to plant new trees when the moon is waxing; that is, when it is growing from new to full. If you are planting by the astrological moon sign, these trees should be planted when the moon is in the sign of Taurus (Riotte, p. 130). Young trees purchased from a local nursery will be leafed, but trees ordered through the mail or parcel service may look like little more than sticks when they arrive. Do not be discouraged by the appearance of these "sticks," and certainly do not assume that your newly delivered trees are dead. The most important part of the tree—what you might think of as its heart and soul—is its roots. If a sapling is shipped with leaves, those leaves are just more mass that the root system needs to support during the journey. After you have planted your little tree (which should be done as soon as possible after it arrives), the roots will begin to gather nourishment and water from the soil, and leaves should soon emerge.

When you plant your tree, be sure to welcome its wood-spirit to your land. Offer it water. You can do this by simply pouring water around the newly planted tree, but since you and the tree will presumably be neighbors for a fairly long time, you might want to put more intention into the act. Fill a clean, attractive pitcher or urn with water and take it out to the tree. First take a sip of the water yourself, saying:

Water is Life.
Blood of Mother Earth, flowing through her arteries
—rivers and streams—
on a journey to the ocean where all Life began.

Now, slowly and gently pour the remaining water around the base of the newly planted tree as you say:

I give you this blessing of Life.
As the Life flows through me,
may Life flow through you.

Finish with your expression of affirmation, as described in the previous chapter. If it feels more appropriate and natural to you, substitute the actual name of the Earth Mother as you know her: Gaia for Hellenic Pagans, Herthe for Saxon Pagans, and so on. As I emphasize throughout this book, your personal rites should be relevant to you and true to the path you follow.

Some of the fruit and nut trees that grow well throughout much of North America include:

- Apples
- Cherries (you will probably need at least two trees of different varieties to produce fruit; I have been told that self-pollinating varieties of cherry have been developed, but I have no personal experience with these)
- Pears
- Plums (you will need two varieties of these also)
- Chinese chestnuts
- Hazelnuts
- Carpathian walnuts

Before ordering trees or purchasing them from a local nursery, find out what fruits and nuts grow well in your region. Any given type of fruit tree may thrive in one area and struggle in another. This does not mean you cannot try a tree that is not known for producing well in your region, but you should be aware of this in advance. As a rule, you will derive more satisfaction from fruit or nut trees that grow well in your area.

A TREE FOR YOUR ALTAR

Many Pagans today like to keep symbols representing a tree on their altars. This is especially true for some druids, and for Pagans following a Saxon or Norse path for whom the symbol represents the World Tree. The symbol can be almost anything, such as a painting or perhaps an iron or an aluminum sculpture. But what could you place on your altar that better represents a tree than…a tree?

When I was a young boy, my grandfather introduced me to the Earth Mother and her wonders. Papa was a Christian, but he had a profound appreciation for the natural world. He and I would spend hours fishing on an ox-bow lake in central Arkansas, where he would tell me about "Mother Earth" as he pointed out the habits of turtles and woodpeckers and gar. Later, when we returned to his home, he would let me help him in his back garden, and there I would have more lessons about the Earth Mother and her ways.

Papa always had an assortment of garden catalogs, and I would peruse these indoors while avoiding the heat of the Arkansas summer afternoons. One thing I often saw in the catalogs that captured my imagination were the bonsai trees marketed (then) as "Ming trees." These were the same miniature trees that are sold in garden centers today: small junipers, with their branches pruned and shaped in graceful curves and their roots confined to a shallow pot. The idea of a tiny tree fascinated me, and that fascination did not diminish appreciably over time.

Many years later, as an adult, I eventually fed my fascination and purchased an evergreen bonsai. I would like to say that my bonsai and I lived happily ever after, but that is not what happened.

The bonsai died.

So I went out and bought a second bonsai. And it died almost as quickly as the first one. Determined, I bought a third. It died. I began to notice a pattern.

After this experience, I gave up trying to keep a miniature tree for years. Obviously, I thought, there must be something fundamentally wrong with me, since I had killed one poor little tree after another. Distancing myself from the idea of having a "Ming tree" gave me some perspective. I realized that I did not really care about bonsai as an art form; I just liked the idea of a tiny tree that I could keep in a pot. As a Pagan, I especially liked the idea of a tree that I could have on my altar.

Eventually I did some more research and found out that there was nothing really wrong with me at all. The problem had been with the tiny trees. Junipers are not indoor plants. I am sure there are some people who have had small potted junipers thriving in their living rooms for decades, but for most of us a juniper cannot be kept indoors, alive, for very long. The juniper bonsai kept by a true bonsai enthusiast is usually kept outside and requires some skill to maintain.

I found some books about indoor bonsai and tried some of the suggested species. Alas, my efforts again resulted in some accidental arboricides. Surely there was some tree that could easily be kept indoors in a pot! (I can be very stubborn at times.) I was looking for a tree—a plant—that could be kept in the house throughout the year.

A tree—a plant—that could be kept in the house. A plant inside the house. Of course! I was looking for a *houseplant*!

Once I realized what I was looking for, I was able to narrow my search down to two species, both of them tropical trees that fare well inside the house: the Ficus (*Ficus benjamina*) and the Schefflera, or "Umbrella Tree" (*Schefflera arboricola*). Either species adapts well as a small, indoor tree suitable for representing the World Tree on your altar or in any sunny location in your home. These tiny trees also make interesting and unusual gifts for your Pagan friends!

To create a tiny representation of the World Tree, you will need a small, young Ficus or Schefflera. You will also need a shallow bonsai bowl. These bowls are sometimes sold at garden centers or can be purchased online. The shallow bowl will limit the depth of the roots. Trees growing in shallow soil naturally remain small. The shallow bowl does not hurt your tree in any measurable way. The tree does not care much whether it is tall or short.

Trim the roots as needed to fit them into the bowl. The tree will look more attractive if you position it slightly to one side of the bowl rather than in the exact center. Pack good-quality potting soil around the roots, and water the pot thoroughly. A layer of aquarium gravel over the top of the soil will help keep the soil in place when you are watering your tiny tree.

Do not hesitate to trim off any branches that look out of place. Beyond that, there is no need to create a "bonsai" form unless you have a personal desire to pursue that art. If so, there are many books about bonsai available. Otherwise, let your tiny tree grow into its own natural look.

If your tree is a Ficus, it will very likely now drop all of its leaves. Do not panic. The new leaves that come in will be smaller and more suitable to the size of your tree. After this, your Ficus will periodically drop its leaves for any number of reasons: if you move the pot, if the lighting changes, or if the tree is just having a bad leaf day. Usually a few leaves will remain through this molting process. Always keep an eye on your Ficus to make sure it has enough water and is not bothered by insect pests or fungi, but do not assume that falling leaves mean your tree is getting ready to die.

Schefflera does not drop leaves in this way. Personally, I like the fallen leaves; it seems more tree-like.

The most important thing to do from here on is to make sure that the pot never completely dries out. This is especially critical during the first week or so, when your tree is adjusting to its new "home." A shallow pot can dry out very quickly, so be sure to check your tree at least every other day. The tree should not be standing in mud, but neither should the soil be completely dry.

Since your tree is in a confined pot, you will need to replenish the soil every two or three years. Carefully remove the tree from its pot. The roots will probably fill the entire interior, leaving very little room for soil. Trim back no more than a third of the root system and repot the tree with fresh, new garden soil. Be sure to tend your tree as carefully as when you first potted it, and be sure to keep the newly trimmed root system moist.

The jade plant (*Crassula ovata*) is a succulent rather than a tree, but if this detail does not bother you, it can be grown as a beautiful living representative of the World Tree. About twenty years ago I had a large potted jade "tree" that elicited compliments from everyone who saw it. You will need to pot your jade plant as you would a Ficus or Schefflera, and then trim off extraneous limbs until the plant resembles a tree with a trunk. Keep the "tree" relatively dry at all times, and give it as much outside time as you can during the summer. Without some direct exposure to the sun, a jade plant can quickly become "leggy" in appearance.

Regardless of species, your tree will need a lot of sunlight to keep it happy and healthy. Only keep it on your altar when you want it there to enhance a ritual, then return it soon afterward to a sunny location in your home. My tiny trees spend most of their time on a low table under a large window so they will be at their best when their presence is required on the altar.

THE BIRDS
AND THE BEES

This holiday is celebrated on the Sunday following the first full moon after the vernal equinox. In Latin it is called Pascha, the French call it Pâques, the Spanish say Pascua, and the Swedes say Påsk. The only two languages that have preserved the name of the goddess who was once praised and honored in mid-spring are German, which names this holiday Ostern, and the English language, where it is known as Easter.

Very little solid information about the goddess Eastre (or Eostre) has survived. Her name is cognate with our word *east*, and so we can surmise that she is a goddess of the dawn and, because of her feast date, of the spring—a goddess of beginnings. Her moon marked the beginning of Eostre's month (Eostremonað), which later came to be known by its Roman name, April. In the pre-Christian era, Eostre's feast was one of the three great festivals of the Germanic world (Jones and Pennick, p. 122).

Popular symbols of Easter such as flowers and newly hatched chicks are essentially symbols of spring. The vernal season must have been very significant for the Anglo-Saxons because English-speaking Christians still use the word Lent (Old English *lencten*, meaning "springtime") in reference to the weeks leading up to Easter. Other languages use a word that translates as "the time of fasting": Fastenzeit (German), Carême (French), Cuaresma (Spanish), and Fastetiden (Norwegian). But during the Middle Ages, when English sermons began to be delivered in the language of the people, the word chosen for the Christians' time of fasting was *lente*, from the Old English *lencten*.

Springtime.

There is no symbol more closely associated with the Easter season than the egg. The official explanation is that eggs represent new life, but an equally important and perhaps more immediate reason why our Pagan ancestors would have associated eggs with springtime is their relative abundance at that time of year (Simpson and Roud, p. 105). The amount of light that chickens are exposed to directly affects egg production. In today's egg "factories," hens are subjected to nearly constant artificial lighting to ensure maximum egg production, but the availability of eggs varied seasonally in earlier societies. In a natural environment, hens begin to lay fewer eggs in the autumn. By the winter solstice, their production has reached its lowest point. As the days begin to grow longer, these same hens start laying more eggs until, by mid-spring, each hen may be producing a new egg every single day.

Imagine what this meant to early Pagan people, especially in northern climates. Fresh food was a luxury reserved for the summer and autumn. By late winter, the village was subsisting on root crops—parsnips and turnips—and old cabbages. Any excess livestock had been butchered in late autumn while there was still grass and enough sunlight for grazing, and meat preservation techniques at that time were less than ideal.

Then came spring's promise. First came the lambing season, which meant fresh milk as the ewes began to lactate. And by this time, the chickens were producing more than an occasional egg. Some eggs had to be reserved for hatching, to ensure another generation of chickens, and these would be placed with brooding hens (which do not lay while they are brooding a clutch of eggs). But there were more eggs left over after enough had been placed under brooding hens, and the additional eggs meant fresh food on the table—symbols of new life, indeed! For early Pagan people, the spring eggs *were* life; they were much-needed sustenance and nourishment after the hardship of winter.

Although Eostre's feast is at the first full moon after the spring equinox, many people today celebrate "Pagan Easter" on the equinox itself. Whenever you celebrate spring, you can connect with your ancestors and express an appreciation for the miracle that sustained them through the years by decorating your own eggs. This is an activity that your whole tribe—your coven or kindred—can participate in together, perhaps on the same day that you give offerings or cast a circle or do whatever it is that your path leads you to do.

If there are children in your group, have a sleepover. The adults can color the eggs at night and then hide them the next morning for the children to find, just as Christian families do. But do not limit yourself to popular custom. Here are some other ideas for your eggs after you have colored them.

In many parts of England before World War II, children would roll hard-boiled eggs down a sloped path or hillside until they broke. They would then eat the cracked eggs. This can be revived as a fun little contest for children. You will need a slope where eggs will easily roll. Each child can select an egg and then take turns rolling these down the slope. The winner is the last child with an uncracked egg.

If you are a Saxon Pagan, color twenty-nine eggs, using a crayon to mark each egg with a Futhorc rune before dyeing it. The wax will repel the dye, leaving the image of the rune on the egg. Place all of the eggs in a basket or large bowl and cover this with a cloth. Invite each person in your inhíred to reach under the cloth and claim one egg. Then read the appropriate passage of the Rune Poem describing that symbol. If the person desires, he or she can accept this mystery by peeling and consuming the egg. If you are not a Saxon Pagan, you can do something similar using the runes of the Elder Futhark or whatever divinatory symbol set is appropriate for your path.

You could also color one egg for each of your ancestors whom you would like to honor. As you begin your spring ritual, place each colored egg on the altar, one at a time, naming the ancestor it represents. After your ritual, take the eggs to some private place outdoors and bury them as personal offerings to your honored ancestors. This obviously is only appropriate if you have your own land. Never bury offerings like this in parks or other public property.

The easiest way to color your eggs is with commercial, chemical dyes. But in the spirit of holistic living, why not try natural dyes? This is not very difficult, and it can be more meaningful than dissolving brightly colored tablets taken from a box with a cartoon bunny on the cover.

NATURAL EGG DYEING

You will need the use of a stove, a pan for each color you want to create, some vinegar, eggs, and whatever fruits or vegetables you will be using for colors. White eggs, of course, are better for coloring than brown eggs.

Here are some common botanicals to choose from:

Ingredient	Color
Violets	Blue-violet
Red cabbage, chopped	Blue
Spinach leaves	Green
Orange peels	Yellow
Ground coffee beans	Brown
Yellow onion skins	Orange
Beets	Pink
Raspberries	Pink or red

There are two primary differences when you dye eggs naturally using the method I give here. First, do not boil the eggs first. You will be boiling the eggs at the same time you are coloring them, so use uncooked eggs. Second, you will dye all eggs of the same color at the same time. That is, instead of dipping one egg in a cup of green dye and one egg in a cup of pink dye, you will color all of your green eggs at the same time and all of your pink eggs at the same time.

Place the eggs you want to dye a particular color in a pan, in a single layer. Cover them with water and add a teaspoon of vinegar. Add your coloring ingredient. There is not a set quantity. More coloring ingredient will create a deeper color.

Put the pan on the stove and bring the water to a boil. Then turn this down to a simmer and let the eggs cook for fifteen minutes. If you cook them much longer than this, they will be tough.

If you are pleased with the color, you may now remove the eggs with a slotted spoon and let them dry. If not, remove the pan from the stove but let the eggs sit in it. If the color of the eggs is still not deep enough after the water has reached room temperature, place the entire pan in the refrigerator and let the eggs sit there in the pan overnight.

Your naturally dyed eggs will not be shiny. If shine is important to you, rub each egg with some vegetable oil.

BACKYARD CHICKENS

I do think seasonal traditions are great fun and add meaning to our lives. But just as I do not want my spirituality to end at the completion of a monthly ritual, I do not want to express it—to live it—only on holidays. And there is no reason why any of us should. Another way you can connect with the earth's natural rhythm and become more fully involved with the cycle of life is by keeping your own chickens.

Even if you live in a city, many municipalities today allow a family to keep several hens. There are usually restrictions as to how many birds you can keep and where they must be located, so check your local ordinances. Those ordinances almost always forbid keeping roosters because of the noise they make. Apparently some people find the pastoral sound of a rooster crowing to be more annoying than distant gunshots, wailing sirens, and screaming neighbors.

Other than the rooster thing, most ordinances are quite reasonable and reflect the basic respect anybody should have for his or her neighbors. But there are exceptions. One Midwestern city currently has an ordinance requiring residents to obtain written permission from every neighbor within one hundred feet of their property if they want to keep a few hens. Other ordinances in this same city address every possible offense—excessive noise, sanitation, and so on—so why the neighbors' permission is required is anybody's guess. Similar written permissions are not required for keeping a macaw or a Rottweiler. It is because of restrictions like this that you must educate yourself about the local laws concerning poultry.

Beyond this, chicken keeping is ridiculously easy. A henhouse for two or three hens need be no larger than a good-size doghouse. The hens will also need some room to run around and stretch their legs, and this area must be securely fenced. Building or buying the henhouse and run will be the most difficult task involved.

And, no, you do not need a rooster. Hens lay eggs whether or not there are roosters strutting around. In fact, you do not want a rooster unless you have a dozen or more hens to keep him distracted. Almost every rooster is insanely amorous and has the nuptial technique of a bulldozer. One rooster will quickly wear down three or four hens to the detriment of their health.

You may be wondering how time-consuming it is to keep a few hens. I have a parakeet in a cage in my living room and three Rhode Island Red hens in a coop in my back yard. Caring for my hens takes up no more time than caring for the parakeet. Both need food and fresh water every day. Both need their enclosures cleaned out once a week, a process that takes me about ten minutes for either the henhouse or the bird cage. There is one significant difference, though.

The chickens feed me.

More than that, they help me connect with the land. They are truly a part of my spiritual experience as a Pagan. I experience, firsthand, what my ancestors experienced when the lengthening days of spring brought an abundance of fresh eggs. I feed my three hens commercially prepared layer pellets, but they supplement their feed with grass and with the bugs in the yard, and so when I eat their eggs I literally become a part of the world around me.

If you decide to keep a couple hens, housing will be your primary challenge. There are websites giving detailed descriptions for building a henhouse, and if you have some reasonable skill with a hammer and saw, this will save you a considerable amount of money. I, unfortunately, do not have that skill. I bought my henhouse. Some assembly will still be required if you choose this option, but none of it is very challenging. The disadvantage of purchasing a pre-built henhouse is that the cost of the structure is comparable to that of a purebred puppy.

As for the size of the structure, the standard rule of thumb is two square feet per hen. The commonsense rule (which I prefer) is "enough room for each hen to be comfortable." You should be able to close the henhouse securely at night. Ideally the henhouse should have at least one small window for ventilation and light, and this needs to be covered with screening. The hens will need a sturdy roost, two inches thick, set at least two feet above the floor. The roost is where they will sleep.

You do not absolutely need nest boxes in your henhouse, but without them the hens will lay their eggs any old place. The egg hunt that is so fun on Easter morning rapidly loses its charm when you have to do it every day. A nest box should be twelve to fourteen inches in width and depth, and should have walls on all sides except the front. Assuming you are keeping no more than two or three hens, two nest boxes are sufficient. If you purchase a pre-constructed henhouse, it will almost always include a roost and nest boxes.

Local ordinances may demand that the chicken run—the fenced-in area where your hens can run around—be located a certain distance from your neighbors' property. In any event, you will want to keep your hens fenced from your garden, at least when you have seedlings coming up. Chickens are not the most graceful creatures. They will scratch and dig and tear up tender young plants. Once those plants are established, though, the hens can be beneficial, nibbling away at insects that would otherwise be nibbling away at your plants.

The henhouse and the chicken run together are referred to as a coop. Like the henhouse, the chicken run should be a secure environment. The fencing must be sturdy. Some people like to have a roof or screening over the run. Why? Because almost *everybody* loves the great taste of chicken. Dogs, raccoons, opossums, hawks, foxes…if it eats meat, it probably likes chicken. Building (or buying) the coop is the most difficult part of keeping hens, but give your birds the most secure shelter you possibly can.

For the same reason, it is a good idea to work protective magic over the coop before or just after introducing your birds. Exactly how you do this will, of course, vary according to your spiritual path. A Saxon Pagan could carry fire—using an oil lantern or a candle protected from drafts—around the coop, saying:

> *Thunor, Red-bearded Guardian,*
> *let nothing be taken or lost.*
> *Keep well the creatures that dwell within;*
> *let them be not harmed.*
> *Cherish them, and let them be not snatched away.*

Thunor is a god of protection, and the wording is taken from an Old English charm to protect livestock. Since the person is asking for Thunor's help, he or she would follow this by pouring a libation of mead or ale.

The stars known to us now as the Pleiades were called "Freya's hens" by the Vikings, so Pagans who follow a Norse path such as Ásatrú or Forn Sed might invoke Freya's protection on a clear, starry night. Roman Pagans might ask Mars to watch over their hens, even as the ancient Romans called on Mars to protect fields of grain.

Plan on keeping two or three hens. Chickens are social creatures. A solitary hen will be lonely and discontent, unless you plan to spend every waking minute with her. Two or more hens will keep each other company and will amuse you with their antics. And two or three hens will probably lay enough eggs for you and your family, unless your chickens are very poor layers or you have a very large family.

In chapter 4 we discussed companion animals as familiar spirits. Your hens probably will not fulfill this role. They are very social, but are not very smart, and they are not inside animals. If your hens are all the same breed, it may be difficult for you to even distinguish one from another.

Some people develop very close relationships with their hens; however, if you are not one of these people, you will still enjoy your birds much more if you relate to them as pets rather than as "farm animals." You will *not* produce eggs more efficiently than professional commercial producers, and you will not save money by producing your own eggs. You will, however, produce more flavorful eggs and derive other benefits, both tangible and intangible, from your pets.

You may discover that the chicken is your personal totem. Chickens, and hens in particular, are associated with both fertility and sacrifice (Andrews, pp. 126–27). Roosters have been considered solar creatures because of their habit of crowing at sunrise, but you will also see a solar connection with your hens as you observe how the hours of sunlight affect their egg laying.

I suggest you provide no additional artificial lighting to stimulate egg production. As I said, you are not going to produce eggs more efficiently than the professionals. If all you want are eggs, just run down to the supermarket and pick up a dozen. On the other hand, if you want to connect with the world, let your hens experience the natural cycle of seasons: the lengthening days in the spring and diminishing daylight in the autumn. Personally, I think this is better for the chickens. I do not mind that my hens go a few days in January without producing an egg. They deserve a break after feeding me all year!

So you have set up a henhouse and chicken run; both of these together are your coop. Now the fun begins! Do you want to get chicks or young layers? There are few things cuter than a baby chick, and chicks are usually easier to obtain than pullets (hens under a year old). Feed stores very often sell baby chicks in the spring. You do not want roosters, so only purchase chicks that have been sexed (examined to determine if they are male or female). Even then, one of your sexed female chicks could mature into a young cockerel! Sexing chicks is not an exact science. The exceptions are a couple of hybrids—the Red Sex Link and the Black Sex Link—that have different-colored male and female chicks, and these may be your best choice if you want to begin with chicks.

Baby chicks are delicate. You will need extra equipment, and they will need extra care to get them through childhood. You will need a brooder, which is a small cage or enclosure where the chicks can be kept free from drafts. You will also need a heat lamp over the cage, and a thermometer. Place the thermometer on the floor of the brooder and raise or lower the heat lamp until the temperature is ninety to ninety-five degrees Fahrenheit, for newly hatched chicks. Each week, for the next four or five weeks, you will need to decrease the temperature five degrees until the temperature in the brooder is the same as the surrounding temperature.

Your chicks will need constant access to water, which should be placed as far as possible from the heat lamp. They will not drink the water if it becomes too warm, and a young chick dehydrates very quickly. They will also need a commercial chick feed. This is usually sold in both medicated and non-medicated varieties. If you are only raising a few chicks, the non-medicated feed should be fine, as the diseases that occur in large farm flocks are less likely to affect your little family of chicks (Kilarski, p. 81).

In my opinion, rearing your own chicks is a lot of work for that little bit of cute you will get in return. Maybe everybody should try it once in their lives, but keeping a small home flock is far easier if you start out with pullets. The problem here is finding someone who will sell a few to you. Farmers are understandably less than eager to sell five-month-old birds that are just beginning to lay. Unless you just happen to know of someone willing to do this, look on the Internet for local farmers with hens they are willing to part with. You do want to look for somebody who seems reliable, because a three-year-old hen looks pretty much the same as a six-month-old pullet to the untrained eye. You will also pay a premium price for a young layer.

Farmers are often happy to get rid of older hens that have started to produce fewer eggs. A chicken lays best for the first couple years and then begins to slow down. The good news is that a hen continues to lay throughout her life, so an older hen may suit you if you do not care how many eggs she is giving you.

The advantages of beginning with pullets or hens are (1) they are much hardier than chicks, (2) you do not need to invest in a brooder and heat lamp, (3) they will begin laying eggs now instead of months from now, and (4) you can be absolutely sure that they are females.

After you've decided whether you want chicks or pullets, you will need to decide what breed or breeds you are interested in. Your selection will be limited by what is available near you, so it is a good idea to have more than one breed in mind. If there are several breeds you like and all are available near you, there is no reason why you cannot have more than one breed of chicken. The hens do not really care; to a chicken, every chicken is just another chicken.

If you live in a warm or mild climate, nothing beats the Leghorn for egg production. These are small, light birds, so they consume less feed per egg than other breeds. Those white eggs you buy at the supermarket almost always come from Leghorns. Because they are light birds, Leghorns are more likely to fly over a fence than heavier breeds, so a roofed enclosure is advised. Leghorns also do not fare as well as other breeds in colder climates.

For brown eggs, some of the best layers are Rhode Island Reds and the Rocks: Plymouth Rocks, Barred Rocks, Partridge Rocks. The Rocks are differentiated by the color of their plumage. All of these are very good layers and tend to be friendly birds. The hens that I now have in my back yard are three Rhode Island Reds whom I have named Henny, Penny, and Jenny. They are always excited to see me, and this spring they were each giving me one egg almost every single day.

I have mentioned the Sex Link hens, which come in both Red and Black varieties. These are also said to be good layers of brown eggs. The Black Sex Link lays a slightly darker egg.

If you can find one, an Araucana hen is a somewhat cautious bird, but a good layer. The interesting thing about this breed is that it produces blue-green "Easter eggs."

There are seemingly countless breeds to choose from, but the ones I have mentioned are some of the best for a small backyard flock. In addition to standard-size chickens, there are bantam chickens, which are smaller and lighter. Their care is almost identical to that of larger hens. Because of their size and light weight, a roofed enclosure is very important and they will fare better in mild or warm climates.

Once you have your pullets—whether you raised them from chicks or purchased young layers—caring for them is simple. Like any animal, they need fresh, clean water every day. Feeding and watering your hens is no more bothersome than feeding and watering a couple of canaries or finches. For food I recommend high-protein layer pellets. I add a little cracked corn, but this is not necessary. The important thing is that your chickens have access to fresh grass and bugs to supplement the feed you give them. When your birds eat grass and bugs, and lay eggs, and you eat those eggs, you take the essence of the land around you into your own body. You become one with the world.

As an added bonus, the grass and bugs are free.

Other than feeding and watering your chickens, the only other routine task you will have is cleaning out the henhouse.

This needs to be done once a week and will take about as long as cleaning a bird cage. A pair of rubber gloves will make this much more pleasant. Before releasing your birds into the coop, you will want to put absorbent bedding in the nest boxes and on the floor of the henhouse. This can be either straw or shredded wood chips. Each week you will need to remove all of this (now mixed with chicken poop) and replace it with clean bedding.

If you also have a garden for herbs or vegetables, cleaning the chicken coop will be a task you will not mind at all. The Earth Mother loves poop, and you will come to love it, too. Well, maybe you will not love it, but you will appreciate it. The dirty bedding you remove from the henhouse is the raw material that can transform your garden into a fertile paradise.

First, the dirty bedding must be composted. Chicken poop has a high nitrogen content and will burn your plants if applied directly to the soil. Composting is just a polite way of saying "making things rot." A compost pile can be as simple as a mound of organic material. My grandfather used to compost his grass clippings in this way, but he had plenty of space for piles of grass clippings and was not in any hurry. The rotting takes place at the center of the pile, so composting goes much faster if you can turn it occasionally and get all the material into the center.

I use a composting drum. These are very convenient, but they are expensive to purchase. If money is an issue, it will cost much less to build a square, three-by-three-foot bin out of used lumber. The bin does not need a bottom; four walls to contain the compost are sufficient. Every week or so you will need to turn the compost with a gardening fork. (With a composting drum, you just turn the crank and the whole drum rolls over.)

Put all the dirty bedding into the compost bin. The straw or shredded wood will rot along with the poop. Also add any weeds you pull from your garden and any vegetable scraps from the kitchen. All of this will decompose and blend together to become the magical ingredient that will cause your garden to flourish. Spread the compost over your garden in the autumn, tilling or digging it into the soil. A second application can be added in the spring before you begin planting.

Beginning around the age of five months, your pullets will begin laying eggs. If your birds have access to grass and bugs, you will probably notice that their eggs taste significantly better than store-bought eggs.

I have been asked at what age a hen stops laying. The answer is that she does not. After a few years, an older hen will lay noticeably fewer eggs, but she will continue to produce throughout her life.

EGG DIVINATION

With your own eggs, you can practice one of the oldest forms of divination. It is a practice known variously as oomantia, ovamancy, oloscopy, or oomancy: "divination with eggs." Some people try this with eggs purchased from the supermarket, but what significance does an egg like that have? You do not know when it was laid or where it came from. It is rather like trying to construct an astrological chart without knowing a person's date or place of birth. When you collect an egg from a nest box, you know exactly when and where it was laid. When you hold the egg laid by one of your own chickens, you hold that moment in time and space when it came into the world.

The ancients had different techniques for practicing divination with eggs, but the method most commonly used today involves the interpretation of the shape that the white of the egg takes when poured into water. To do this, heat a cauldron with fresh water. If you do not have a cauldron, any contemporary cooking pot will suffice. That is what a cauldron is, after all: a medieval pot.

Select an egg laid that same day, and pray to a god or goddess of your spiritual path for guidance. I pray to Woden, who is a master of divination and magic among the Saxon deities. After your prayer, carefully break open the egg and separate the white from the yolk.

Remove the cauldron from the fire or stove. The water should be hot, but not boiling. Slowly pour the egg white into the water. The white will be clear when you pour it, but will quickly become white (which is why it is called the "white") and take on shapes as it cooks in the hot water. Like cumulus clouds on a summer day, some of the shapes will remind you of objects or creatures. Ignore meaningless wisps of egg white, and note only those shapes that seem to resemble something.

Egg divination is like crystal gazing in that it is extremely subjective. A shape may mean one thing to you and something entirely different to someone else, and the same shape may mean different things to you at different times. The shape of a serpent, for example, could mean danger (if you are afraid of snakes), or renewal (because a snake emerges from its old skin), or good health (especially for Hellenic Pagans, for whom the snake is a symbol of healing). The shape of a hammer could equally represent either construction or destruction, because a hammer can be used to build something or to break something apart. When you note a significant shape, consider what that shape means to you *at that very moment.*

What you do with the leftover yolk is your own business. If the omen was good, you may want to cook the yolk and eat it, taking the blessing into yourself. Obviously you do not want to do this if the omen was not so good.

NECTAR OF THE GODS

Keeping two or three chickens is easy, but it does require a few minutes from you each day. If you want to go out of town, even for a weekend, you will need to make arrangements for somebody to feed and water your chickens and collect the eggs. If this is more than what you want to commit yourself to, there is another animal even easier to keep that can connect you with the earth's cycles. No "livestock" of any kind demands less attention than the honeybee!

As with chickens, many municipalities permit residents to keep a hive of honeybees. Amateur beekeepers can be found in some of our largest cities.

You might be thinking, "But they are creepy bugs!" Yes, and they are creepy bugs that can sting you. For this reason, if no other, it is a good idea to take a beekeeping class before getting actively involved in this hobby. There is nothing intuitive (from our human perspective) about insect behavior. You know what it means when a dog snarls, but can you tell what a honeybee is likely to do? When a chicken is sick, you will usually notice that something is wrong; however, without some basic education, you can stare at an entire hive of dying bees and think they are doing fine.

Why keep bees? There are a few excellent reasons:

- Honey. (We might as well start with the obvious.) If you brew mead—a fermented honey wine—there is nothing so nice as using your own honey. Jars of your honey also make great Yuletide presents for coven members, coworkers, and friends.

- Beeswax. The caps from your honeycomb can be saved when you collect your honey. These can be melted down and made into ritual candles (a subject we will be discussing in chapter 9).

- To connect with the earth's cycles. Beekeeping is yet another way to sharpen your awareness of the world around you. Although bees are very low-maintenance, you may need to provide them with water during a drought. You will look forward to warm, sunny days when it is easiest to approach the hive. Every change in the environment will take on deeper significance for you.

- Pollination. Fruit trees and many other flowering plants need bees to help carry their pollen from flower to flower.

- Entertainment. Keeping a hive of bees is much like owning a miniature city! The more you learn about your bees, the more you will come to appreciate them. Each bee in your "city" will have his or her own duties. Some will be responsible for comb construction, while others will manufacture beeswax. Some will air-condition the hive in the summer, others will care for the young, and still others will stand guard at the hive entrance. Although bees need very little attention, you may find yourself "checking the hive" just for the fun of seeing what your bees are up to.

- A beekeeper can be the life of any party. For most people, beekeeping is an exotic and interesting subject. It is sort of like being an astronaut or a rock star, but with far less work.

By keeping a hive of bees, you can have a complex and thriving matriarchy in your own back yard. Your mini-metropolis can have a population exceeding fifty thousand honeybees, but ultimately only one of them—the queen—is really important in the grand scheme of things. For your hive, the queen truly is the Great Mother. All the other bees are quite literally her children. The majority of these are hard-working daughters who raise younger siblings for the good of the hive and who store honey both for themselves and for you. (To be perfectly honest, though, they are not really doing anything for you. Domestic bees store far more honey than they actually need, but the only reason you are not breaking the law when you steal that extra honey is because it is we humans who make the law.)

A minority of the bees in your hive will be sons, male bees, who do not do much of anything. It is not because they are lazy; they simply are not equipped to do anything. Male bees (drones) cannot even sting. In the autumn, their sisters drive them from the hive, after which they soon die. There is probably some kind of moral lesson here.

Beekeeping is one of humankind's oldest industries, dating back to 2000 BCE or earlier. The first hives were probably made of logs (Ambrose, p. 4). Early beekeepers approached honeybees as sentient and responsive beings, and this attitude continued well into the Christian era. In an eleventh-century Anglo-Saxon manuscript, a charm to capture a swarm of bees instructs the beekeeper to say:

> *Sitte ge, sigewif, sigað to eorðan!*
> *Næfre ge wilde to wuda fleogan.*

In this charm, the beekeeper addresses the swarming bees as "war-women" *(sigewif)* and commands them to settle to the ground. The beekeeper does not call upon a deity or some other supernatural entity to control the bees. Instead, he speaks to the bees directly, saying: "Settle ye, war-women, sink to the ground! Never should you, wild, to the wood fly" (Griffiths, pp. 195–96).

Folk tradition called for the beekeeper to share the news of any important family events—births, deaths, marriages—with his bees. To fail to do so was to invite bad fortune. The beehive, which is itself a complex community, was considered an integral part of the greater community.

As a totem animal, the honeybee is symbolic of both fertility and productivity (Andrews, p. 337). Bees are sacred to both Artemis and Demeter, to Apollo, and to the Egyptian god Ra. Honeybees may have exceptional totemic significance for Pagans who follow a strong Mother Goddess tradition. The honeybee's stinger is sometimes considered a phallic symbol, which is ironic since only the females—workers and queens—have this accessory.

One of the best ways to find a beekeeping class is to contact one of the many beekeepers associations found throughout the United States. If the association does not offer classes, they can very likely direct you to somebody who does. They may also have other activities (workshops, lectures) that you can participate in.

Getting set up initially will be your biggest investment in both time and money. Obviously you will need a hive. I recommend the traditional Langstroth movable-frame hive. Proponents say that some new, innovative hive designs are superior alternatives to the Langstroth hive, and there may be some merit to these claims, but there are certainly disadvantages to using an experimental design. The Langstroth hive has been in common use since 1861, and has been introduced to all parts of the world (Ambrose, p. 13). The majority of beekeepers you meet will be familiar only with the Langstroth hive, and supplies for repairing and maintaining this design are readily available from beekeeping supply companies.

You will probably have to order your hive, and when it arrives, you will need to assemble it. The wooden pieces will be pre-cut and only need to be nailed together. This is not especially difficult; if you can assemble a plastic model, you can put a hive together.

The Langstroth hive consists of box-shaped components called "supers." Your kit will probably include two large supers, also known as hive bodies, which will eventually house the queen, workers, and drones of your colony. (In some regions, a single hive body is considered sufficient. This will be addressed in your local beekeeping class.) More shallow supers are for your bees to store their excess honey in. These will be added to your hive as needed. In addition to the supers, the hive should have a bottom board, a queen excluder, an inner cover, and an outer cover. Hive kits often include a small wooden stand.

In your beekeeping class, you will learn about other necessary equipment: the hive tool (a sort of miniature crowbar), the smoker, protective clothing, the bee brush, a feeder, and extracting equipment. Most of this you will buy, but try to find somebody who will let you rent an extractor and an uncapping knife. You will only need these one day each year, so it does not make sense to purchase them. Conversely, a professional beekeeper will have extracting equipment sitting around useless for most of the year and can make a little extra cash by renting it to the hobby beekeeper. If you do find a beekeeper who will rent you the extracting equipment you need, be sure to return it in pristine condition!

Ideally your beekeeping class will have at least one hands-on session where you can work directly with live bees and get past the "creepy bugs" prejudice that so many people suffer from. This is extremely important to do *before* a package of ten thousand honeybees arrives at your post office. Your instructor, an experienced beekeeper, will show you how to approach the hive, use a smoker, and handle frames without freaking out.

You will order your bees from a supplier. If the variety of breeds confuses you, just order Italian bees. It is a very popular breed, and the bees are relatively docile. I also like Buckfast bees, but I think every beekeeper has his or her favorite variety. The bees will typically come as a "package," and you will need a queen of the same variety. In fact, as I said earlier, the queen is really the only bee who matters. If Her Royal Majesty is a Buckfast, it does not matter that you ordered a package of Italians; in a couple months, you will have a hive populated entirely with Buckfast bees.

Your bees will arrive in the spring when the temperatures are warm enough to ship them safely. While waiting for the little ladies to make their debut, you can work protective magic over the hive itself. Be sure to approach this in a way that will exert a calming influence over the bees that will be residing within the hive.

You may want to ask for the protection of a god or goddess of your tradition who takes a special interest in bees or honey. As a Saxon Pagan, I would ask this of Ing Fréa. The Hellenic Pagan would pray to either Artemis or Demeter, depending on whom he or she has a closer relationship with. A Kemetic (Egyptian) Pagan could appeal to Ra.

Whether using magic or prayer—or a combination of both—do *not* burn incense inside or close to the hive. The scent that you find pleasantly appealing could be a source of acute irritation to the honeybees who will eventually inhabit the hive.

When your bees finally do arrive, you will probably need to pick them up at the post office. They will be in a box with screening on two sides to provide ventilation. The queen is usually packaged in the box in a special little cage of her own. By this time you will have set your hive up outside and finished your beekeeping classes. You should know how to install the bees in their new home.

Let me share a secret with you here. Your bees did not take the same beekeeping class that you did, nor did they bother to read any books about beekeeping. They are going to do whatever they please, without a care for what humans write or teach about them. So do not be caught by surprise when your bees do not follow a prescribed behavior.

I learned this when I set up my first hive back in the 1990s. I hung the queen in her cage between two frames in the hive body, as I had been instructed. Then I mixed water and honey, and sprayed the box of bees with this mixture so they would "easily pour" into the hive. Up to that point, everything had gone according to the plan. Then I very carefully pried open the box, and the plan was discarded. There was no pouring involved. Instead I suddenly had a swarm of thousands of bees flying around me in a dark, humming cloud. I think about twenty bees actually managed to pour into the hive. Their 9,980 sisters decided to fly about the yard instead. But I had the queen safely in the hive and, as I have said, she is the one bee who really matters. By nightfall, all (or at least most) of the bees had entered the hive and were busy organizing themselves.

Your experience will very likely be similar. After the initial period of panic (both for you and your bees) while you get them established, they will settle down, and eventually you will too. Always remember that your queen *is* the hive. If she is doing well, then the hive is probably doing okay. And once the little ladies have settled in, they pretty much take care of themselves. You will need to medicate them for the few diseases that afflict honeybees (your beekeeping instructor will go over this with you), and you will probably want to feed them in the early spring and occasionally check to make sure that Her Royal Majesty is attending to her perpetual egg-laying duties. You will have to care for the hive a bit in the spring and then harvest the honey in the fall, but between these two periods there really is not much to do. The bees will feed themselves throughout most of the year and take care of their own sanitation needs.

What more could you ask for?

Even if you do not want to care for your own birds or bees, you can still connect with the creatures that live around you. Plant to provide food and habitats for the birds. Pyrocantha, holly, barberry, privet, and coralberry are all good choices. Plant pussy willow or a redbud tree to provide early spring food for the honeybees, or seed your lawn with white clover. In recent years, the honeybees of North America have suffered from colony collapse disorder, so they can use all the help you can give. It is very likely that any honeybees who visit your garden are in fact domestic bees belonging to a beekeeper who lives within a couple miles, so you will also be helping out a human neighbor.

But whether the bees you provide with pollen and nectar are domestic or feral, the nature spirits will undoubtedly be pleased and the land around you will more readily flourish.

CHAPTER EIGHT

MAKING FOOD

Quite a few Pagans, including Wiccans, Celtic Pagans, Saxon Pagans, and ADF druids, observe a high summer holiday at the end of July or in early August (in the Northern Hemisphere) celebrating in one way or another the first grain harvests. The Gaelic name for this holiday is Lughnasadh, and it honors the memory of Tailtiu, the foster mother of the Irish god Lugh. Lughnasadh is the name favored by Pagans who follow most Celtic paths, although a Welsh Pagan may prefer the Welsh name Calan Awst ("the August gathering"). The Saxon name for the holiday is Lammas, from the Old English *hláfmæsse*, meaning "loaf festival." This name is favored by Pagans who follow Germanic-inspired paths such as Fyrn Sidu or Seax Wicca.

The name Lammas tells us something about this holiday. It was a celebration not so much of grain, but of the bread that can be made from grain. Fruits and vegetables can be picked and eaten as they come off the plants, but the fact is that much of our food has to be *made*. Butter, cheese, bread, wine, and jam do not grow on trees. Even the foods that do not need to be made, foods that come ready to eat right off the vine, often need to be preserved in some way. Vegetable crops do not deliver their goods in precise, meal-size proportions; the vegetables ripen all at once over a relatively short period of time. As I write this, my kitchen counter is piled with zucchini and yellow squash that will have to be preserved to prevent them from rotting.

By making and preserving food, you can connect with your Paleo-Pagan ancestors and develop a deeper appreciation for the miracle of the sustenance we receive from the soil beneath our feet. For Pagan people, activities like this become even more meaningful when they are sacralized and incorporated into our ritual calendars.

Traditionally, in northern Europe, bread was baked with a combination of grains, but wheat flour was always included to supply gluten to the dough, and wheat was harvested earlier than the "poorer sorts" of grain (Hartley, pp. 184–85). Wheat is typically ready to harvest around the summer solstice, although the exact time depends on the weather conditions in any given year. But ripened wheat is not ready to be consumed. Once it was harvested, the wheat was allowed to dry. The wheat was then threshed to separate the grains from the chaff, and then winnowed to actually remove the chaff, and finally ground between stones to produce a usable flour.

All of this took time in pre-industrial societies. When the wheat corns had finally become wheat flour, people were ready to celebrate Lammas, or Calan Awst, or whatever late summer holiday was observed in their respective cultures.

I am not suggesting that you reenact this entire process, from planting the wheat to baking the bread, although you certainly could if you were so inspired. Two Pagans in Missouri, a brother and sister, do just this. The brother (with the support of his lovely wife) plants the wheat and harvests it, and the sister grinds some of the harvested wheat and bakes it into loaves of bread. Through each annual cycle of sowing and reaping, these two siblings and their families experience, hands-on, the Earth Mother's divine mysteries of death and rebirth. Together they intentionally follow a Hal Sidu, a holistic tradition.

EASY-PEASY LAMMAS LOAVES

For most Americans today, taking wheat on its journey from seed to loaf would be quite an adventure. For many, just transforming flour into bread is a challenge. But in our modern world of conveniences, you can still celebrate a "loaf festival" even if you have no idea how to bake bread and even less desire to learn. In the freezer section at most supermarkets, you can find pre-made, unbaked frozen bread dough. This is portioned into "loaves" so even the most unskilled cook can place a loaf in a pan, put it in the oven at the prescribed temperature, and remove a beautiful, fresh loaf of bread twenty to thirty minutes later. But you are not going to follow the directions—at least not exactly as given on the package.

When Lammas approaches—near the end of July for those of us in the Northern Hemisphere, or the end of January south of the equator—purchase enough frozen bread dough for your entire coven or kindred, keeping in mind that a little dough will rise into a surprising amount of bread. Set the dough in your refrigerator the night before your people will gather for their late summer celebration.

By the following day, the dough should be thawed. Now the fun begins. You can cut a "loaf" in half or in thirds, or twist two together to create a super-size loaf. You are not going to bake your Lammas loaves in standard bread pans, so the sizes and shapes are almost limitless. Try slicing a loaf into three equal-size strips and braiding them together. Shape a loaf to resemble a person or some kind of animal. (Hint: When molding human and animal shapes, make them very skinny. The bread bodies will thicken considerably as the dough rises.) Your loaves can take the shape of suns, crescent moons, or spirals—whatever you are inspired to fashion.

Furthermore, your Lammas loaves do not need to be plain wheat bread. Before shaping a loaf, you can knead in chopped nuts or cinnamon and raisins. Here again, you are limited only by your imagination.

Instead of using bread pans, bake your Lammas loaves on cookie sheets. Spray or wipe the cookie sheet with oil before putting the dough on it. I find it is easier to prepare and shape the dough before placing it on the cookie sheet.

Now you will need to wait for the dough to rise. Since it has already thawed, this should take no more than two or three hours. Preheat your oven to the temperature given on the package. When the loaves stop rising, put the cookie sheets in the oven. The time given on the package presumes you are baking pre-portioned loaves of dough. If you have created larger or smaller loaves, you will need to adjust the time accordingly. Check the baking loaves frequently after the first fifteen minutes. When the outside of a loaf is brown and crusty, it is done.

You can bake these easy Lammas loaves yourself, but this is an activity that everyone in your kindred will enjoy. Even children can join in the fun of making small Lammas loaves in an array of shapes and flavors. Have a contest to see who can create the most interesting or attractive loaf. The results of your labor can be part of a Lammas feast or given as offerings to your gods, or both.

FROM FLOUR TO LOAF: A SIMPLE QUICK BREAD

If you want the experience of making bread from "scratch" but have little or no baking experience, try a quick bread. This is bread that rises as it bakes without using yeast. Compared to yeast bread, a quick bread is very easy to make.

You will need self-rising flour, sugar, and a twelve-ounce can of beer. Be sure you have *self-rising* flour; it will be described this way on the packaging. As for the beer, any variety will do, but a full-flavored beer will result in tastier bread. When making quick bread, avoid any beer with the word *Lite* in its name.

Preheat your oven to 350 degrees F. While the oven is heating, sift together 3 cups self-rising flour with ⅛ cup sugar. Open the can of beer and pour it into the dry ingredients, stirring it in thoroughly. (There is no reason you cannot use bottled beer. What matters is the quantity: 12 liquid ounces, no more, no less.) Put the mixture in a bread pan or on a cookie sheet and bake for 35 minutes.

That is all there is to it. Quick breads are so easy, you might wonder why anyone would resort to using frozen dough for their Lammas loaves. There are two reasons. Not everyone likes quick bread. It is considerably heavier than yeast bread. The second reason is that it cannot be readily shaped the way frozen dough (after it is thawed) can. Nevertheless, there is a satisfaction of baking your own loaf of bread from scratch, even when the recipe is as simple as a quick bread.

Eventually you may even want to try your hand at baking yeast breads. For the novice, learning how to make bread can seem like the equivalent of earning a four-year college degree, but it really is not all that difficult after you have had a little practice.

Lammas seems the most obvious time to bake bread as an expression of your spirituality, but, depending on your path, there may be other seasons when this can be equally or even more meaningful. I also bake at least one loaf at the opposite season of the year, during the late winter festival known variously as Imbolc, Candlemas, or Ewemeolc. The early Saxons offered "sol-cakes," or mud-cakes. The cakes themselves were not made of mud, of course; they were buried or tilled into the muddy earth as offerings. I usually make a quick bread using oatmeal for my sol-cake offering. (*Sol* is an Old English word meaning "mud" or "wet sand." Since early English scribes were Christian, the Latin word *sol*, meaning "sun," often appears in Anglo-Saxon manuscripts. In the context of sol-cakes, however, it is much more likely that the early English people would have used their native word *sunne* if they had thought of these offerings as "sun-cakes.")

SOL-CAKES

We do not know how the early Pagan Saxons made their sol-cakes, and the following recipe is obviously quite modern. After all, the early English people had neither quick cooking oats nor brown sugar! This is also more complicated than the previous quick bread recipe, but the combination of oatmeal and wheat flour may more closely approximate the multi-grain breads of pre-Christian Europe.

You will need the following ingredients:

1 cup milk

1 ¼ cups quick cooking oats (uncooked)

2 eggs, beaten

1 stick butter, melted

½ cup light brown sugar

2 cups all-purpose flour

2 ¼ teaspoons baking powder

½ teaspoon salt

Preheat your oven to 350 degrees F. and grease a bread pan. Combine the milk and 1 cup oats in a large bowl, stirring these together thoroughly. Add the beaten eggs, melted butter, and brown sugar. In a separate bowl combine the flour, baking powder, and salt. Add this dry mixture to the first bowl and mix well.

Pour the resulting batter into the prepared bread pan. Sprinkle the remaining ¼ cup of oats over the top of the batter. Bake for 1 hour.

This cake can be used as an offering by people who follow almost any Pagan path. Wiccans can use it as a delicious sabbat cake.

PUTTING FOOD BY

If you have produced a portion of your own food in even a moderate-size vegetable garden, you have already developed an awareness of a challenge that our Paleo-Pagan ancestors were continually confronted with: the Earth Mother does not deliver her bounty in daily portions. At the beginning of this chapter, I mentioned the pile of zucchini and yellow squash in my kitchen. In one afternoon I chopped and froze twenty quarts and then went outside to bring in almost as many new squash. Baskets of corn have also come in from the garden, and there is a limit to how much corn I can eat at one meal. Now we are waiting for the tomatoes.

How much simpler it would be if a head of lettuce, two tomatoes, a zucchini, and two ears of corn—and nothing more—would be ready to pick on a given day! Alas, if we are to have an intimate connection with the earth, we must accept that we are only one small part in the grand scheme of life. Mother Earth is not our servant. Her bounty is delivered to us in its own time, and it is up to us to preserve what we cannot consume. Otherwise we can only watch helplessly as the excess rots away.

Even if you do not have the time or desire to grow your own vegetables, preserving food is a useful tool for nurturing your connection with the earth. Farmers offer locally grown produce throughout the summer months at farmers' markets and roadside stands across most of the United States. When you eat locally grown food, you literally become a part of your environment by taking the bounty of the land around you into your body. On a less esoteric level, you also support your local economy! The only problem is the same that confronts Pagans who are growing food in their own back yards: any given food becomes ripe and available all at once at the same time of year.

When shopping at a farmers' market, do not assume that the produce is locally grown. Ask questions, and be specific in phrasing those questions. "Fresh" is a vague term. For that matter, so is "local." Where exactly was the produce grown? When was it picked? Educate yourself so you know when specific crops are in season in your region. The people who sell produce at farmers' markets are like any other businesspeople: some are highly ethical, others not so much. To some extent, you will need to trust the seller, but it is good to know something about the vegetables you intend to purchase.

There are also no ethical prerequisites for operating a roadside stand, but you can generally assume that the vegetables sold really are locally grown. Still, ask the seller where and when the product was harvested. Most farmers will appreciate your interest, and you will learn more about where your food has come from.

Perhaps the easiest way for the twenty-first century Pagan to preserve food is simply by freezing it. This is admittedly not an ancient tradition, but it certainly would have been if our ancestors had possessed the technology to build electric-powered freezers. Cryogenically storing food is the best way to preserve nutrients that might otherwise be lost.

Enzymes in frozen vegetables can cause the color, texture, and flavor to break down. This is avoided by blanching the vegetables before freezing them. Blanching is an easy process of boiling or steaming the vegetables for a few minutes. Whether or not you choose to do this will depend on how and when you intend to use the vegetable. I never blanch my summer squash because I use it in chili and casseroles where the color and flavor disappear in the dish anyway. However, if the appearance and texture of the vegetable are important, or if the vegetable will be kept frozen for more than two months, blanching is recommended.

Before blanching and freezing—for that matter, before beginning any process of preserving your food—you might want to ask for the aid and guidance of a protective deity. As with all things, which deity this is varies according to your spiritual path. For me, the god Thunor is the most logical choice. I believe that prayer should come from the heart and not be recited like a magical incantation, but my words usually go something like this:

Thunor, strongest of gods,
ward this food and keep it safe.
Let no hob nor púca foul these gifts of the earth.
As the fare remains hale,
so I shall ever honor you with due faith.

Blanch each variety of vegetable separately. Cut the vegetables into even-size pieces no more than one or two inches across. Use about one gallon of water for every pound of vegetables. Bring the water to a boil before putting the vegetables in. The easiest way to blanch your vegetables is to place them in a metal basket and then lower this into the boiling water. Start counting blanching time as soon as the water begins boiling again.

The length of blanching time varies depending on the vegetable:

- Green beans. Three minutes. You can blanch the whole beans or cut them into pieces, whichever you prefer.
- Broccoli. Three minutes. Cut into 1½-inch pieces.
- Carrots. Two minutes. These can be diced, cut into slices, or into sticks, depending on your preference.
- Corn. Four minutes. Blanch the entire ears and then cut the kernels off afterward. If you want to preserve it intact as "corn on the cob," blanch medium-size ears for about nine minutes. Add or subtract two minutes from this if the ears are especially large or small.
- Okra. Four minutes.
- Sweet peppers. Two minutes. Cut into strips.
- Summer squash. Three minutes.

You will also need a second pot of cold water (60 degrees or less) to plunge the vegetables into just after you have pulled them from the boiling water. This is done to stop the cooking process immediately. Put a handful of ice cubes in a pot of water to make sure it is cold enough. The cooling time is the same as a vegetable's blanching time.

After cooling, let the vegetables drain thoroughly before sealing them in plastic freezer bags.

Not all vegetables lend themselves to freezing. This includes anything that is not cooked before consuming. Lettuce is a good example of this. Even without blanching, frozen lettuce will be wilted and mushy when it thaws out.

The best time to preserve any vegetables, whether by freezing or canning, is when the moon is waning (decreasing from a full moon to the dark of the moon).

CANNING

Although more complicated than freezing, canning has its own advantages as a method of food preservation. Canned foods can be stored literally for years, and there is no danger of losing the rewards of your labor due to a lengthy power outage.

There are two canning processes: pressure canning and water bath canning. Pressure canning requires a special piece of equipment—a pressure canner—and is more difficult. If you find that you enjoy canning, then pressure canning is something you might want to explore, but water bath canning is better for beginners. The disadvantage of water bath canning is that it is only suitable for vegetables with a high acid content. The good news is that a high-acid vegetable is one of the most popular foods grown in American gardens: the tomato!

To can tomatoes, you will need the following items:

- A water bath canner. This is basically a large pot with a metal rack insert for holding jars.
- A large, ordinary pot. This is for scalding and then cooking your tomatoes.

- Canning jars. These are available at most supermarkets. They come in pint and quart sizes. The quart jars are more economical. Be sure to get *wide-mouth* jars. Your canning jars can be used over and over.
- Canning lids. These are flat lids with a rubbery rim. They can only be used once, but they are very inexpensive.
- Canning rings. Like the jars, the metal bands that secure the lids in place can be used over and over.
- A jar grabber. This looks sort of like a wide set of tongs. It is used to lift the jars out of the boiling water. You should be able to get this at the supermarket also.
- A ladle.
- A canning funnel. This is optional.
- Lots of tomatoes. You should have twenty pounds or more. (If you do not have enough from your own garden, buy more from local farmers.)

The first thing you will need to do is peel your tomatoes. Fill the large (ordinary) pot halfway with water, and bring this to a boil. Add as many tomatoes as you can, and boil them for three minutes. Drain the boiled tomatoes, then put them in cold water. You can use another pot for this, but I just fill a clean kitchen sink with water and add a few ice cubes.

Peel the tomatoes. Scalding them will have loosened the skin, so this is easier than it sounds. As you peel the tomatoes, cut them into quarters and put the pieces back into the pot that you boiled them in, but this time without any water. Save the peels for your compost!

While doing this, you can also be sterilizing your canning jars. Your dishwasher may have a sterilization cycle. This works fine, but alternately you can fill the canner with water, bring the water to a boil, and sterilize your jars in that. They should remain in the boiling water for about ten minutes.

After you have peeled the tomatoes, take a moment to pray for aid and guidance from a protective deity, as described earlier for freezing vegetables.

Now bring the pot of tomato pieces to a simmer, stirring frequently. The tomatoes should simmer for ten minutes. It is very important to stir the tomatoes or they will stick to the bottom and burn.

Your tomatoes are now ready to can! Using a ladle, fill each jar carefully. Here you will discover why I recommend only using wide-mouth jars. No matter how careful you are, at least some of the tomatoes will spill. (A canning funnel is not absolutely necessary, but it will make this part of the process much easier.) Wipe the top and sides of each jar with a clean towel. After this, put ½ teaspoon salt in each quart jar (¼ teaspoon if you are using pint jars). Put the lid on the jar and screw this down *loosely* with a canning ring.

Put as many jars in the canner as it will hold, and cover these completely with water. Bring this to a boil. Let boil for a full ten minutes.

Using the jar grabber, very carefully lift each jar out of the canner and place on a table or counter. Let the jars cool at room temperature. During the cooling process, you will hear popping sounds as the jars seal themselves. When you put the lids on the jars, you will have noticed that each lid has a slight hump (called a dome) in the center. After the lid "pops," this hump disappears and the lid becomes flat and smooth.

The popping means that the jars are properly sealed. After they have cooled, feel the lids to make sure each one has flattened and sealed. If a lid still has its hump, the jar did not seal. This does not mean there is anything wrong with the tomatoes; it only means that they must be refrigerated and eaten soon, just as if you had opened that jar. Now screw the canning ring down tightly on each sealed jar.

Canned tomatoes are great for making marinara sauce, chili, or salsa. Best of all, the tomatoes came from your own land (or at least from land near your residence).

MAKING JAM

If you are growing any soft fruits (strawberries, blueberries, and so on), it is easy to make your own homemade jam. If you are not growing any soft fruits, maybe local farmers are selling them. You will need:

- A water bath canner.
- A large pot.
- A large, solid (not slotted) metal spoon.
- Canning jars, lids, and rings. For jam, I recommend smaller jars. A quart of jam goes a long way!
- A jar grabber.
- A ladle.
- Soft fruit.
- Sugar.
- Lemon juice.

As with canning, the best time to make jam is when the moon is waning.

First, crush the fruit. You can use a blender or food processor, but some people believe this lessens the flavor. Crushing the fruit with a potato masher works just fine. Meanwhile, sterilize your jars. (See the previous section on canning for directions.)

Stir 1 cup crushed fruit together with 1 cup sugar and 1 tablespoon lemon juice. Put this into the large pot. The pot will seem oversized, but the jam is going to froth as it cooks. If you are using something extremely large, like a good-size stock pot, you can double the amount of fruit, sugar, and lemon juice.

Bring this slowly to a boil over medium heat, and stir frequently. After it comes to a boil, reduce the heat to maintain a gentle boil. In other words, bubbles should be coming up, but it shouldn't look like the thing is going to explode. Stir occasionally to ensure that it does not burn. Run the spoon through the jam and lift it, letting the jam drip off. Notice how it drips off the spoon.

It is important to familiarize yourself with how the jam drips, because you are going to monitor it as it cooks to see how it is thickening. Periodically run the spoon through the jam and let it drip off. When the jam is ready, it will start to thicken, and the drops will come together to pour off the spoon as a solid sheet or a single big gob.

Remove the jam from the stove, and use your spoon to skim off the foam. The foam can be discarded.

Using this method, you will need to make several batches of jam to make it worthwhile to seal the jars in your bath canner. Ladle the hot jam into each jar, then put on the canning lids and screw them down with the rings. When you have enough jars to seal, put sufficient water in your canner to completely cover the jars (but do not put the jars in yet) and bring this to a boil. When the water is boiling, put the jars of jam in the metal rack and lower this into the canner. Let the jars boil for a full fifteen minutes.

Finally, use the jar grabber to lift each jar out of the canner. Let them cool at room temperature. As with canning tomatoes, listen for the popping sounds as the jars seal themselves, and make sure each jar is fully and properly sealed.

MEAD MAKING

While we are on the subject of food-related crafts, I should mention mead making. Mead is a fermented honey beverage that was once a popular drink throughout Europe, especially in northern climates. Saxons, Ásatrúar, and other Pagans who follow northern traditions (including many Celtic Pagans) offer mead as a libation in our rites. In my book *Travels Through Middle Earth: The Path of a Saxon Pagan*, I devoted an entire chapter to the process of mead making. Your local wine-making supply shop probably offers other excellent books on mead and can offer personalized advice.

Making mead can be a fun and rewarding experience for anyone, but for the Pagan who keeps a hive of bees it is almost an imperative! A single hive can easily produce fifty to a hundred pounds of honey in one year. In a good year the beekeeper might pull 150 or more pounds of honey from the hive. That is going to sweeten a lot of biscuits. After eating as much honey as they can, using it in baked goods, sweetening enough tea to fill an Olympic-size pool, and giving away jars of honey as Yuletide presents, most Pagan beekeepers will still have plenty of honey left over to experiment with mead making.

Whether using your own honey or buying it from a supplier, begin brewing when the moon is waning. If you observe astrological (zodiac) signs, the best time is when the moon is in one of the water signs: Cancer, Scorpio, or Pisces.

BUTTER FOR IMBOLC

Many Pagans celebrate a holiday at the first of February. For Saxon Pagans this holiday is called Ewemeolc, Irish Pagans call it Imbolc, and still others know it as Candlemas. Whatever the name, the celebration takes place on or near February 2nd (or for those living in the Southern Hemisphere, August 2nd) and is one of the eight seasonal festivals in the Wheel of the Year observed by most Pagans today.

This holiday means different things to different people. In the Irish calendar, the second day of February is the Feast of Saint Brigid, one of the Christian patron saints of Ireland. Many Pagans who follow Irish and other Celtic traditions believe that Saint Brigid is one and the same as the older, indigenous northern goddess known variously as Brigid, Bride, Brighid, Brigantia, and Brigindona. The assumption is that since Saint Brigid is revered by Gaelic Christians in early February, then the goddess Brigid must have been revered during this same season. Whether or not this is true does not diminish the meaning of Imbolc for the Pagans who make offerings to this goddess.

The name Candlemas is also Christian in origin, and unrelated to the Feast of Saint Brigid. Candlemas celebrates the presentation of the child Jesus at the Temple of Jerusalem. According to the Bible, Joseph and Mary took their son to the temple forty days after his birth in accordance with the Law of Moses (Luke 2:22–40). Because of its name, Candlemas is sometimes confused with Saint Lucia's Day, which is traditionally associated with a procession led by a girl wearing a crown of candles. But Saint Lucia's Day occurs in December, not early February. Nevertheless, for many Pagans today, Candlemas is a celebration of candles, representing the "returning light" as the days grow longer.

Ewemeolc and Imbolc are names meaning "ewe's milk," in reference to the lactation of female sheep that begins shortly before the lambing season. Ewemeolc is a Saxon name, while Imbolc is Gaelic in origin. (Depending on your source, Imbolc is also sometimes interpreted as meaning "in the belly," still in reference to the gestation of ewes.) For our pre-Christian ancestors in northern Europe, ewe's milk was the first fresh food available after long weeks of subsisting on old cabbages, root crops, and heavily salted meats. Moreover, lactation heralded the birth of the new lambs that were so important to the northern economy. Sheep were the very foundation of prosperity for the early English people (Hartley, p. 129). Sheep provided not only wool and mutton, but also leather hides, ram's horns for elaborate drinking cups, lanolin secreted around the ewe's neck and udder, and tallow from fat, which was used as a lubricant and later for making candles. And, of course, sheep provided milk and its byproducts, cheese and butter.

I have heard some Pagans say that the lactation of sheep has no meaning or significance to them since we can now purchase fresh milk and an endless array of other foods at our supermarkets throughout the year. But the same can be said for the "returning light" in an era when the flick of a switch can fill a room with artificial daylight in the middle of the night. The lengthening days are important, but the theme of lactation is just as meaningful to the seasonal celebration of Imbolc. If you have any northern European ancestry in your pedigree, you might not be here at all to read these words if it were not for the lactation of ewes. This miracle—and it really is nothing short of a miracle—helped our ancestors survive long enough to produce another generation of men and women to carry on, and then another, until at last you and I were brought into this world. And that, I think, is cause enough for celebration.

Imbolc (or Ewemeolc or Candlemas) is a traditional time to seek omens, especially in relation to the weather. The American tradition of Groundhog Day—waiting to observe whether the groundhog sees its shadow, which supposedly foretells whether there will be six more weeks of winter— came from older European customs of watching other animals such as badgers or snakes. Celebrations often involved specific foods: butter, milk, and a flat, scone-like bread called a bannock.

These same foods can be incorporated into your own seasonal celebration. We Saxon Pagans usually honor our gods and ancestors with offerings of mead, but at this time of year my inhíred gives an offering of whole milk. It is the Saxon custom to share what is being offered, much as you might share a meal with close friends, and so we each drink as we give thanks for the miracle that allowed our ancestors to survive. The remainder of the milk is then shared with our gods as a libation.

I say we use whole milk in our Ewemeolc rites, but even this is not as "whole" as milk is when it comes from the cow; most of the butterfat has already been removed. Whole milk has a fat content of only 3.2 percent (in contrast to 2 percent milk, which, of course, has a fat content of 2 percent). The remaining butterfat is separated into cream that can have a 20 percent or better fat content. Heavy whipping cream has a 36 percent butterfat content.

Butterfat, as you have probably surmised, is the primary constituent of butter. Butter can be made from sheep's milk or goat's milk, but almost all butter consumed in the United States is made from the butterfat produced by cattle.

Making your own butter at home is a great project to engage in with your children during the Imbolc season. The wondrous, almost mystical transformation from liquid cream to a semi-solid butter fascinates most children and can be used as a catalyst for family conversations addressing the transformative events that can and do affect each of us. The death of a loved one, the end of a friendship, even the awkward subject of puberty—any of these transformations may be easier to discuss while changing cream into butter. The change can be a metaphor for the many transformations we experience throughout life.

Not that you need any special issues to address! Butter is just plain fun to make, and surprisingly easy. Even if you do not have any children in your inhíred or coven or kindred, making butter at Imbolc will engage the child within you. Making butter is a rewarding experience for people of all ages.

To make your Imbolc butter, you will need a pint of heavy whipping cream, a quart jar with a lid, a mixing bowl, and a spatula or large spoon. I use an empty, clean mayonnaise jar, but a leftover canning jar with its lid and rim will work just as well.

Pour the heavy cream into the jar. You can add a pinch or two of salt, but this is not really necessary. (I never add salt.) Put the lid on the jar, and make sure it is screwed on tight. If you are doing this alone, go wherever you keep your television and put in a DVD that you enjoy. Making butter is easy, but it can be sort of boring if you do not have friends or family to interact with.

Now shake the jar. Use a steady up-and-down motion, but do not worry whether or not you are doing it "correctly." There is no easy way to do this wrong. Shake the jar, and then shake it some more, and then keep shaking it. A steady, rhythmic movement will be less tiring for you than frantically shaking it like a lioness trying to kill her prey.

You might think this is a modern innovation compared to the wooden plunge churn used in the Middle Ages; however, the method I describe here is actually the older technique for making butter. The earliest butter churns were devised fifteen hundred years ago, but people had been making butter for twenty-five centuries before that! Early butter making was often accomplished by placing sheep's milk or goat's milk in a skin bag and then shaking it. I suppose to be completely authentic you could try to make a skin bag, but I recommend the quart jar.

In addition to keeping a steady motion, shake the jar with only one hand, because this hand is sure to become exhausted and you will need your other hand ready to take over the task.

Keep shaking. I said this was easy; I did not say it was quick.

After a while, solid bits will begin to form in the cream. This is a good sign, but keep on shaking. Do not stop to examine the creamy bits.

When you think nothing is ever going to happen (and possibly even a little while after this thought has crossed your mind), the cream will suddenly and almost miraculously separate into a solid lump of butter sitting in the remaining liquid.

Pour off the liquid and put the lump of butter in the mixing bowl. Using your spatula or large spoon, bring the lump up the side of the bowl and press out any liquid that is still in it. After pressing out the liquid, your fresh butter is ready to eat. This can be used as part of an Imbolc feast, or a portion can be offered to your gods and ancestors.

CHAPTER NINE

PAGAN CRAFTS

In the last chapter we looked at expressing Pagan spirituality through food-related crafts. The activities discussed in this next chapter are, at best, only indirectly related to food. Most of these home activities are seasonal and fit very well into the contemporary Pagan Wheel of the Year.

CANDLE MAKING

Candles have become an integral part of contemporary Pagan rites. We Pagans routinely use candles to illuminate our altars. Wiccans place candles at the four cardinal points around the perimeter of their ritual areas. ADF druids will light a candle as a symbolic representation of the celestial realm. Pagan sorcerers of all traditions—whether drýmenn or mágoi or streghe— very often use candles as they work their magic.

You can purchase candles for whatever purpose you intend, of course, but ritual and magical tools are so much more potent when we put a little of our own energy into their creation. Candle making is something you can do alone or as a coven or inhired activity. Older children often enjoy making ritual candles with adult supervision. This activity is a great tradition to bring into your life, and there is no better time for making candles than at Candlemas.

There is a practical side to making candles at Candlemas, since this is usually the coldest time of the year for those of us who live in temperate climates. (If you are using a Catholic calendar and live in the Southern Hemisphere, Candlemas will be the warmest time of the year, but this book is intended for Pagans who will presumably invert their holidays when living or visiting south of the equator.) Candle making involves a hot stove and hot wax, and can continue for hours on end if you have the supplies and enthusiasm to keep going. If you do not mind paying an exorbitant electric bill for air conditioning, you can make candles on the hottest day of summer, but it just makes more sense to melt wax and pour candles when the heat this generates will help warm your home, lower your furnace bill, and have a minimal negative impact on the environment.

If you practice candle magic, whatever your spiritual path may be, there is a very good reason for making your own candles beyond putting your own energy into creating them. I often come across spells instructing me to continue meditating or chanting or at least continue sitting in front of a candle until it has burned completely down. This can be impractical, to say the least, when using anything larger than a tea candle, and it can often be difficult to find tea candles in any color other than basic white.

Unless you make your own.

When making your own candles, you also have complete control over what goes into them. You control the exact color. You control the scent, if any. Make a candle with a contagious link to yourself or another person by cutting a little bit of that person's hair (or your own) into tiny pieces and mixing it with the wax. Make a protective candle by sprinkling a pinch of iron filings into the melted wax. (Magically speaking, iron is a protective metal, which is one reason why iron horseshoes are considered "lucky.")

There are countless books and websites with instructions for making all sorts of candles, plain or fancy, but the basic process is really quite simple. You will need the following equipment and supplies to make candles. Depending on your expertise and personal desires, you may want a lot more, but this is an essential list for making simple candles:

- A heat source. Usually a stove, but a hot plate will suffice.
- A large, low pot for boiling water.
- A smaller pot that will easily fit into the large pot for a double-boiler arrangement. For the small pot, check out thrift stores. You will be melting wax in this, which will likely ruin it for other purposes.
- Paraffin wax. You can buy the little boxes sold in grocery stores for canning, but this is not the best variety for making candles, and the cost per pound of wax is relatively high. Look at hobby shops or online for paraffin wax sold in eleven-pound slabs. (If you keep bees, the wax cappings removed from your honey frames can be melted to make beautiful beeswax candles.)

- Wicks. These sometimes come with a thin zinc or tin "core" running through the wick to help keep it straight while you are making candles. The metal core burns away as the candle burns. Cored wick may be a little easier for the novice to work with, but it is not essential by any means.

- A container or mold to pour the wax into. Container candles are by far the easiest candles to make when you are first starting out. Small, ordinary jelly jars can be used to make pretty container candles.

The first thing to do is to set your wick in the mold or container. It is important that the wick be centered. Tie the top of the wick around a small rod of some kind (I have even used pencils to hold the wicks in place), clip the wick to the depth of the container, and then lower the wick into the container or mold until the rod rests on the container's rim. Shops that sell candle-making supplies often have clay or special tabs to hold the bottom of the wick in place. These are not absolutely necessary, but they can be helpful.

Put a couple inches of water in the large, low pot that will serve as the bottom of your double-boiler arrangement. Heat this on the stove. Meanwhile, break chunks of wax from your paraffin wax slab, and put these into the smaller pot. When the water on the stove (or hot plate) begins to boil, place this smaller pot into the large pot. Do *not* attempt to melt your wax directly on a stove or hot plate. This is extremely dangerous, as paraffin wax can burst into flame if it gets too hot. Always melt your wax with the double-boiler arrangement. The bottom pot of water ensures that your wax will not be heated above 212 degrees F., the boiling point of water.

When the paraffin wax melts, it will become a crystal-clear liquid. At this time you can add color or fragrance if you wish. This is also when you should add any magic enhancements, such as the aforementioned hair or iron filings. Use only a minimal amount of these substances, as they can affect how the candle burns, and not always in a good way. Some substances can even be toxic when burned. Use common sense and know what you are burning in your candles!

Candle-making supply shops sell both colors and fragrances embedded in small wax chips that can be added to your melted paraffin. As an alternative, you can add color simply by removing the paper wrap from a crayon and then dropping the crayon, or a part of it, into the paraffin. The advantage is the wider range of colors you can find in a large box of crayons. The disadvantage is the clarity of color, which is often pale in comparison to the rich, deep colors achieved with color chips.

If you do not want to use scent chips, using essential oils is another way to add fragrance to your candles. An essential oil is extracted directly from an herb or sometimes from an animal gland (as with civet oil, for example). In contrast to this, a fragrance oil is a synthetic product. Unlike true essential oils, fragrance oils do not always have the same scent when burned, so I do not recommend them for candle making. Using essential oils to add scent is trickier than using a crayon to add color. The problem is that the oils evaporate and disperse quickly when heated. If you want to try this technique, add some oil to your melted wax just before you pour it into the container or mold. Soaking the wick in the same essential oil before setting it into the mold will also help preserve the scent in your candle.

When the wax is melted and you have added any color or fragrance you have chosen, you are ready to pour your candle. Be very careful while doing this. The wax is hot! It is unlikely that you will suffer any permanent injury if you spill wax on yourself, but I guarantee it will not be a pleasant experience. It is also a good idea to spread newspapers or a tarp over any surface where you will be pouring wax. No matter how careful you are, some of it will probably dribble, and getting hardened wax out of carpeting is no picnic.

Pour the melted wax into your container or mold, reserving a portion of it for a second pouring. Do not overfill the container. After pouring the wax, check to see that the wick is still centered. If it is not, move the wick until it is centered again, being careful not to spill any hot wax on you.

Now let the wax slowly cool. As it cools, the wax will contract, leaving a dimple in the center of the candle. In a large candle, this dimple can be quite deep. This is why you have reserved some of your wax for a second pouring. After the candle has fully cooled, reheat your reserve wax and pour this into the dimple. You may even need a third pouring. This is less important for candles poured into molds because the dimple will be at the bottom of the candle where you cannot see it. Nevertheless, you may want to fill in a large dimple rather than have a molded candle with a gaping hollow in the base.

After the second (or third) pouring, let the candle completely cool for several hours or even overnight. If you have used a mold, be sure to wait until the wax is fully solid before attempting to remove the candle. It is disheartening to have a candle come apart as you pull it from a mold because the inner portion was still warm and soft.

The final step, whether you have used a mold or a container, is to trim the wick to about a quarter inch in length. You now have a candle suitable for use in a ritual or spell.

There is no reason why you cannot make just one candle, but you will find that it is much more efficient to make a larger number of candles at the same time. In fact, you may decide to make all of your annual ritual and magic candles at Candlemas!

The complete control you have over your choice of color, size, scent, shape, and other factors might be overwhelming when you first attempt to make candles. First consider the purpose of the candles. Will they be used for worship, or do you want candles primarily for casting spells? Candles used for worship can be used again and again. Repeated use can even imbue your ritual candles with deeper meaning. If you are making ritual candles for your altar or, if you are Wiccan, directional candles to place at the cardinal points of your circle, larger candles will last for months and possibly throughout the entire year.

Candles such as these can even be "eternal." After a full year's use, most of the altar candle (or quarter candle) will have melted away. Break up the remaining wax into chunks, being careful to remove any wicking, and then melt these pieces while adding fresh wax to make up for the lost volume. You can then pour a renewed candle that contains the essence of the previous year's candle. If the candle was dyed or scented, you will of course want to add more color or scent to the melted wax before pouring it.

If you are using beeswax—and a warm, burning beeswax candle is a sensory delight—it will be more difficult to add color or scent because the wax already has its own natural color and aroma. Beeswax is best for ritual candles that need no color or scent enhancement. Like paraffin ritual candles, a large beeswax candle can last most or all of the year.

On the other hand, if the candles are intended for spell casting, then smaller candles usually make more sense. Most sorcerers, Pagan or not, do not want to use candles that carry a resonance from earlier spellwork. For this reason, a candle that is used for magic is usually a one-shot item. There is no point in pouring a tall, thick candle if you are going to throw it out after a single use, and it makes even less sense if the spell requires you to be present until the candle completely burns out.

Whether making candles for worship or for spellwork, consider your spiritual path when choosing colors and scents. For myself and other Saxon Pagans, red is a color of power. In the practice of magic, the Law of Sympathy states that two things that resemble each other share similar properties. Red is the color of blood, and blood represents life and vitality; ergo the color red represents life and vitality. For this reason, red objects are often used in Saxon and other Germanic magic. As you might expect, I always keep a supply of small red candles on hand for spellwork. However, if you follow a Hellenic, Kemetic, or Celtic path, your own tradition may favor other colors.

Some tried-and-true spells require candles of particular colors. You can never anticipate all of your needs, but if you know that you have a favorite spell requiring three yellow candles, then it makes sense to pour some small yellow candles for future use.

When designing your own spells, here are some colors that tend to be associated with specific intentions:

- Red, as I have said, is a color of life and vitality because it is the color of blood. In magic, it can be thought of as the color of physical (animal) life and all things associated with that, such as strength and health. This is the color for sex magic, although some people claim that red-orange or pink candles are more effective. Pink is essentially just a lighter shade of red.

- Yellow is often associated with knowledge, mental clarity, and communication. Yellow candles can be used in spells intended to help a person study and retain knowledge. Yellow is also a color of friendship, perhaps because good communication is essential between friends.

- Gold candles are good for prosperity spells because (of course) they are the color of gold. This is another example of the Law of Sympathy.

- Silver candles, too, are good for prosperity, for the same reason as gold candles.

- Green, being the color of chlorophyll, is the color of plant life. Green candles are useful for horticultural spells. In the United States, a green candle is just as likely to be used in a prosperity spell, since green is the color of American paper currency.

- Blue is a color of the emotions and the subconscious. Blue candles can be used in spells directed toward spirituality, emotional balance, or developing psychic skills.

- White represents purity and cleanliness. Because of these qualities, white candles are often used in spells for healing or protection.

These color associations are generalizations. As always, consider your spiritual path. Kemetic Pagans, for example, should be aware that the ancient Egyptians associated the color white with death. Likewise, in some cultures the color green is associated with sickness and misfortune. Just as we do not all communicate verbally in the same language, we do not all share the same magical language!

For ritual candles used in worship, the choice of color will usually be entirely subjective since you are not using the candles to evoke specific energies. For altar candles, unless your spiritual path decrees otherwise, it is best to let your heart be your guide. We have three ritual candles on our household altar: one to honor our gods and goddesses, one to honor our ancestors, and one to honor the elves (natural or worldly spirits). The colors of these candles change from one year to the next, the only criterion being what appeals to my hired-menn and me at the time. This may work for you, too, or you may prefer specific colors for your altar candles. Wiccans very often use specific colors to represent the elements around the perimeter of the ritual area: green for earth, blue for water, yellow for air, and red for fire.

JOHN BARLEYCORN

He stands in our garden, leaning slightly back with his gaze lifted to the heavens, his arms joyfully outstretched. It looks as if he might burst into song at any moment. His shirt is faded, and there is a hole in his jeans. I am conscious of him standing near as I gather a basket of squash and golden ears of corn. He has stood in that same position since May Day, and will continue to hold vigil there throughout the rest of the summer and autumn.

I am talking about the effigy of John Barleycorn, a scarecrow that my inhíred builds each year as a representation of the life of the field. I have been doing this for twenty years now. I was building scarecrows before Earendel Inhíred existed, before I moved east to Pennsylvania. The tradition of John Barleycorn has been a part of my life for a long time.

Today, for me and my folk, that tradition has become well defined through years of repetition. When we first gather for May Day, we build a scarecrow as a part of our rite welcoming the beginning of summer. One of us sews up John Barleycorn's head, while somebody else brings and assembles the wood framework for his body. Everyone helps, and everyone critiques our collective progress as we fill out John's glutes, thighs, and biceps with handfuls of straw. After the scarecrow is built, each person comes forward with a small piece of cloth that he or she has embroidered one or more runes on. The runes convey what that person hopes to bring into his or her own life through the coming summer. You could say that the runes represent what that person hopes to "harvest." These rune cloths are then carefully stitched to John Barleycorn's garments. After this, the scarecrow is paraded to a garden where he will stand until October's moon grows full.

Last year John Barleycorn stood in the back garden at the home of two of my híredmenn. This year I am fortunate to have him here.

Scarecrows have been around for a long time and have been associated with Pagan spirituality for almost as long. Around twenty-five hundred years ago, Greek farmers carved wooden scarecrows in the image of the god Priapus, the son of Dionysus and Aphrodite. The scarecrow that my tribe builds represents John Barleycorn, who is not actually a god, but a personification of the harvest. He is also the subject of an old English folk song.

A summer scarecrow is inexpensive to build. Here is what you will need:

- A seven- or eight-foot-long wooden pole
- A second, shorter pole, about three feet in length
- Nails
- An old shirt and a pair of long pants
- A hat (discount stores often sell cheap wicker hats in the spring)
- An old pillowcase, sheet, or some other scrap cloth
- A needle and some sturdy thread (quilting thread works well)
- Scissors
- Bale of straw

The trickiest part of this is making the head. Cut two pieces of cloth in the shape of a head from the pillowcase or sheet. Make this a little larger than your own head, and leave a long "neck" at the bottom. The neck can be unnaturally long, as any excess length will be hidden in the scarecrow's chest.

Stitch the two cloths together, leaving the bottom of the neck open to stuff straw in. After you have done this, turn the "head" inside out. This will hide the stitching. At this point it will look less like a head and more like a limp sack. If you wish, you can paint or embroider eyes or other facial features on the head piece.

Next, assemble the framework for the body. Using a couple of nails, fasten your poles together in a cruciform arrangement. The shorter pole will be the "arms" of your scarecrow, while the long pole will support the neck, body, and one of the legs. The extra length of the longer pole is to allow you to bury the bottom in the ground. You want John Barleycorn to stand up, of course!

Pull the pants onto the framework, drawing the bottom of the longer pole through one pants leg. After this, put the shirt on over the framework arms. Now, using your sturdy thread, put a stitch through the back of the pants and shirt where they come together at the waist. The back of the shirt should be inside the pants as you do this. This stitch is just to help hold the clothing in place.

Pull the "head" over the top of the longer pole. Tuck the neck inside the shirt, and then put a stitch through the back of the shirt and neck. Leave the front of the shirt open for now.

You are now ready to begin stuffing your scarecrow. One bale of straw is much more than you will need, but that is how it is sold. Use the leftover straw to mulch your garden.

Begin by stuffing the extremities: the legs, the arms, and the head. Several people can be doing this at the same time, with one person filling up the head while somebody else stuffs straw down the pants legs, and still another person stuffs the shirt arms. You may want to tie off the ankles of the pants and wrists of the shirt with lengths of twine to help hold the straw inside the clothing.

When the extremities are packed with straw and well shaped, fill the chest cavity. Button up the shirt, leaving only the top two or three buttons unfastened. Close these off after you have stuffed the chest.

Finally, give John Barleycorn his hat. You will want to fasten this to the head with a couple more stitches. Even if the hat seems secure, it can disappear with the first high winds if it is not stitched to the head.

If you do not yet have an inhíred or coven, if there is no tribe to celebrate with, then building a six-foot-tall straw man might be a little too ambitious. A smaller scarecrow can be made using children's clothing or even doll clothing.

Does your garden consist of a few pots of herbs and leaf lettuce on your apartment balcony? Buy a shirt and pants ensemble for a twelve-inch male fashion doll and make a micro-scarecrow. Instead of buying a bale of straw, stuff the little guy with a few handfuls of dried grass.

I mentioned earlier that my híredmenn affix runes to the scarecrow every spring. This is our own custom. Any customs or practices involving your scarecrow should be meaningful to you and relevant to your spiritual tradition. We also let John Barleycorn stand in different gardens so everyone has a chance to have him for a summer, but your group may not want to do this. You may have a special site considered to be holy and sacred for all of your kinsmen, and prefer to set up the scarecrow there every year.

At the end of the year, we also have a custom for disposing of the scarecrow. We use a lunar calendar, so our end-of-summer rite takes place when the Winterfylleth moon grows full, which is almost always in October. Celtic Pagans might want to do this at Samhain.

Just as our scarecrow is "born" at the beginning of summer, he "dies" at the beginning of winter. We set up a small pyre in a fire pit, and John Barleycorn is placed in a standing position over this. Following a ritual in which we honor and praise our ancestors, we set the pyre ablaze and offer John Barleycorn to our gods.

In many urban areas, burning a straw man in your back yard is likely to bring the police to your house. Make sure you are not breaking any laws.

SOLSTICE WHEELS

Celebrate Midsummer by making a sun wheel! This is a northern European symbol of good fortune, related to the fylfot and the Brigid's cross. The swastika is a form of this symbol that fell out of favor after it was conscripted by the Nazis and used as an emblem for their regime.

The sun wheel is an equal-armed cross inside a circle:

Just as the scarecrow can be created and displayed in different ways, so can this solar image. Have your coven or kindred build a large sun wheel and burn it as an offering on a Midsummer bonfire. (As with the scarecrow, be sure it is legal to do this in your neighborhood.) Or have everybody create personal sun wheels to keep on household altars. Or have a contest to see who can craft the most attractive sun wheel. Or, by yourself, make sun wheels to give to your friends and family as Midsummer gifts.

I could go on and on like this, but you get the general idea.

If you have a talent for craftsmanship, you can gather vines and build your sun wheel from scratch. But not all of us have that degree of talent, so instead I am going to tell you the easy way to make a sun wheel.

Begin with a grapevine wreath that can be purchased at any well-stocked craft store. This will be the circle of your sun wheel. That is the easy part. Now you have to go out and find some wild vines.

Or maybe not. While you are at the craft store buying your wicker wreath, look around to see if they have anything that can be used for the equal-armed cross. We have used grape-vine ribbon, or you can twist several lengths of round basket-weaving reeds together. The material used for the cross of your sun wheel needs to be moderately flexible but stiff enough to hold its shape.

If your local craft store does not have anything suitable, wild vines work very well. We usually use wild vines because (1) they are free, and (2) they grow like weeds in western Pennsylvania. On the other hand, purchasing reeds or ribbons from your craft supply store may be easier than foraging for vines if you live in a desert region or in downtown Manhattan.

Whatever the central cross will be made of, use narrow cloth ribbon to tie the vertical and horizontal pieces together. Then weave the four ends of the cross into the grapevine wreath at equidistant points, and tie these in place with more ribbon.

If you wish, you can decorate your sun wheel with even more ribbons, feathers, and colorful dried flowers.

MAKING SCENTS

Most Pagan people use incense in their rites, and those who practice magic may also make use of other forms of aromatics. The word incense comes from the Latin *incendere*, meaning "to burn," for incense is a blend of aromatic substances intended to release a fragrance as it smolders. These aromatics are herbs and other plant materials, often blended with a small amount of essential oil.

Commercial incense sold in the form of cones or sticks has been combined with a binding agent to hold its shape, and usually with another substance to ensure that it burns easily. The name of a commercial incense may describe its dominant aromatic (lavender incense, patchouli incense), but just as often it will be marketed with an exotic name, such as Jungle Love or April Rain. The popular Indian incense known as Nag Champa is a combination of frangipani and sandalwood.

The one advantage of commercial cones and sticks is their convenience. Strike a match to the end of the incense and your part is done. But when we put little effort or thought into our actions, the reward is equally meager. Making your own incense is rewarding and places you in greater control of what aromatics you are burning.

In my opinion, the best way to make your own incense is to prepare it as loose incense. Loose incense is nothing more or less than cone or stick incense without the extraneous binding and burning ingredients added. It consists entirely of the aromatics, finely ground and blended together however you choose. You do not need to do anything special to it because the loose incense is burned over a charcoal sold in small packages at almost every New Age shop in the United States. These charcoals can also be purchased at Christian religious supply stores.

By now you know that the aromatics you choose to burn in votive rites should be appropriate for your spiritual path. Saxon Pagans, for example, might burn mugwort because this herb is sacred to Woden. Roman, Hellenic, or Kemetic Pagans might choose to burn frankincense, which was popular throughout the Mediterranean area in early Europe for thousands of years.

Rosemary is an appropriate aromatic for almost any European spiritual tradition. Native to the Mediterranean region, rosemary was introduced across Europe by the Romans.

When making incense, always grind your aromatics to a fine powder. In powdered form, they can be blended with other aromatics more easily and will burn more evenly. If using a resin such as frankincense, it is a good idea to purchase it in powdered form. Resins are hardened tree sap and are extremely difficult to grind into powder. If you must powder resin, put it in the freezer for half an hour first, and grind it with a mortar and pestle, never in a mechanical grinder.

Used by itself, a resin need not be powdered. Resin grains will melt and release their odor as they warm on the charcoal.

But much of the enjoyment of making incense is in creating your own unique blends. After mixing together whatever powdered herbs or flowers you want in your incense, you can add a few drops of a compatible essential oil. This is optional. If you add oil, be sure that it is a true essential oil and not a synthetic fragrance oil. The latter does not always smell the same when it burns. The essential oil should be used very sparingly; do not let it overpower the scent of the other aromatics.

A word of caution here: Some botanicals are toxic when burned. You are safe using aromatics that are found in any kitchen spice cabinet (rosemary, cinnamon, sweet basil) or that are commonly used for incense (sandalwood, frankincense). If you are unsure about a leaf or flower, research it in a comprehensive herbal such as Lesley Bremness's *The Complete Book of Herbs* or Paul Beyerl's excellent *The Master Book of Herbalism*.

There are many books available with incense recipes you might like to try. In my opinion, the best book ever written for beginners is Scott Cunningham's *Magical Herbalism*. Even if you only want to make incense for votive rituals and have absolutely no interest in magic, the book is a valuable resource. I especially like his simple Meditation Incense (p. 120).

After decades of working with herbs and incenses, I have collected and developed quite a few recipes. Most are magical blends, but the recipes I give here can be used equally well for votive rituals.

Success Incense
4 parts cinnamon
2 parts powdered sandalwood
2 parts powdered frankincense
1 part powdered orris root

This can be used when working any spell to bring success or prosperity into your life. Because of its nature, it is also a suitable incense to burn as a praise offering to your gods.

Frith (Peace) Incense

2 parts lavender blossoms
2 parts violet blossoms
1 part powdered orris root
1 part finely grated lemon peel
1 part crushed cardamom pods

As a magical incense, use this when working spells to create peaceful conditions and dispel chaos.

Healing Incense

4 parts powdered sandalwood
4 parts carnation petals
2 parts bayberry leaves
2 parts rose petals
1 part saltpeter

The purpose of this incense is implicit in its name, but refrain from burning this or any other incense directly in the presence of a sick person, especially if that person's respiratory system is compromised.

Uncrossing Incense

2 parts lavender blossoms
2 parts rose petals
2 parts verbena
1 part bay leaves

Burn this incense to remove any spell that has been cast against you. I honestly do not think this happens very often; in my experience, most sorcerers who waste a lot of time "cursing" people are not competent enough to concern yourself with. Nevertheless, this is a good blend to have on hand if you believe that something like that may have occurred. Because of the intent of this incense, it can be a suitable votive offering to gods or spirits associated with protection.

Attraction Incense

8 parts powdered olibanum

4 parts powdered sandalwood

4 parts cinnamon

2 parts powdered myrrh

2 parts powdered orris root

1 part saltpeter

Use this in love spells intended to attract potential partners (rather than one specific person). This blend comes from a Book of Shadows that I inherited from a witch who passed from this world many years ago. I have found that the incense also works well as a votive offering for gods or spirits associated with love and sensuality.

After powdering and blending your chosen aromatics, the loose incense is ready to burn. To do this, take a small metal or ceramic bowl and fill it partially with either salt or sand to insulate the bottom. The Anglo-Saxons called a bowl such as this a *recelsfæt*, or "incense vessel."

Unless your ritual room is the size of a cathedral, you will not need to use an entire charcoal. Break the charcoal in half, or even quarter it, and use only a portion. Light the charcoal and set it into the bowl.

Now sprinkle your loose incense onto the coal. Any incense you want to keep for later use should be stored in an airtight container in a cool, dark place.

Incense Cones

If you want to try making your blend into incense cones, you will also need gum arabic and saltpeter (potassium nitrate). Making incense cones can be messy. I personally prefer to blend and use loose incense. With that disclaimer, here is what you need to do to make incense cones.

Mix 1 teaspoon of gum arabic in 8 ounces of water. This should form a thick paste. If it is dry, add a little more water. Then cover this with a warm, damp cloth and set it aside.

Sift your loose incense, using only the finest powder. If necessary, grind it up some more.

Weigh the sifted incense. A good kitchen scale is accurate enough for this.

Add 10 percent (by weight) saltpeter to your sifted incense. Mix the saltpeter in thoroughly.

Now begin adding the gum arabic mixture to your incense a little bit at a time. Blend it in completely before adding more. Continue adding this in, slowly, until your incense dough reaches the consistency of modeling clay. Squeeze some in your hand to see if it will hold its shape.

Mold the dough by hand into the same size and shape of incense cones sold commercially. If the cones are too thick, they will not burn properly.

Place the shaped cones on waxed paper, and let them dry for a week in a warm, dry room.

POTPOURRI

You do not have to burn your aromatics to enjoy them. Gift shops and bath shops often sell aromatics in the form of potpourri, which is even easier to make. A potpourri of chopped cedar twigs, pieces of rosemary, orange rind, cinnamon sticks, allspice, and a little vanilla oil can add a fragrant dimension to your Yuletide altar. Or set out a potpourri of sweet woodruff, violets, and dried rose petals for May Day. For either one, adding a little salt will help preserve the mixture. Orris root powder is also a good fixative.

Making a potpourri is very similar to making incense, only easier. Since the aromatics will not be burned, there is no reason to powder them. Dried flowers, herbs, spices, and even fruits can be used for potpourri. Any attractive bowl or snifter can be used to hold the finished product.

Put potpourri into a little cloth bag, and that bag becomes a sachet. These are often used to scent closets and drawers, but they are also useful for the Pagan sorcerer. Sachets can hold protective herbs, healing herbs, love herbs, or herbal blends for almost any other purpose. Tuck a sachet of protective herbs under the seat of your car to help keep you safe on the road. Place a sachet of lavender blossoms and mint leaves inside your pillowcase to promote peaceful dreams.

If you are a merchant, keep a sachet stuffed with mint, thyme, and chamomile in your cash box to help you enjoy the sweet smell of success.

CORN DOLLS

After you have celebrated Lammas (or Lughnasadh or Calan Awst), when you are harvesting the bounty of your garden, you can honor the spirits of the land by making a corn doll. In principle, corn dolls are similar to the John Barleycorn scarecrow, only they are smaller and made entirely of plant material rather than being stuffed with straw. The corn doll can be thought of as an idol representing the life of the land.

Traditional English corn "dolls" were not always dolls. They were often crafted in nonhumanoid forms, such as a bell (Essex and Cambridgeshire), a lantern (Norfolk), a pretzel-shaped knot (Stafford), a horseshoe (Suffolk), or a spiral (Yorkshire). In Scandinavia, they were often shaped to resemble stars or crowns.

Furthermore, they were never made from the husks of what we Americans call corn, because this is a New World grain that was unknown in Europe until the sixteenth century. Although in the United States the word corn has come to be a synonym for maize, it actually means any kind of seed. Thus the seed of the oak tree is called an acorn (oak-corn). In England, the word corn refers to any grain: wheat, barley, rye, oats.

Nevertheless, the husks of corn (maize) are great for making corn dolls. The instructions I am giving here are for making a humanoid corn doll using corn husks. You will need string, scissors, and, of course, the corn husks.

This will be a much more meaningful activity if the corn came out of your own soil, but if you didn't plant corn, you can pick up a few ears at your farmers' market. For that matter, you can even buy those dried husks sold at craft stores, but you will have to soak these in water to make them pliable. The other disadvantage of dried craft husks is that they probably were not grown in your area and thus have no connection with the local land spirits.

You will need at least six husks to make a doll. Hold four or five husks together in a bundle, and tie one end of this together tightly with a piece of string. Cut off any excess string.

Now turn the bundle upside down and gently pull the long ends of the husks down over the tied-off shorter ends. Pull them down on all sides: front, back, left, and right. Be careful not to break any of the husks as you do this. When you have pulled the long ends down, tie them with a string to form a "head" and "neck," with the rest of the husks hanging down as a sort of loose yet unformed "body."

Now take one or two other husks and roll them as tightly as you can lengthwise. Tie the ends with string (you may need to tie the middle also). This piece will be the "arms" of your doll.

Fit the arm piece through the long husks, just below the neck of the doll, so it protrudes from each side like a pair of arms. Tie another string around the body below the arms to create a "waist."

You can stop here if you wish, or you can embellish the doll further. If you would like a fuller skirt, tie another four or five husks from the waist of the doll. Alternately, you can give the doll legs by dividing the husks below the waist into two bundles, tying them at the "knees" and "ankles."

The corn doll can sit proudly on your harvest altar. Keep it somewhere in your home throughout the winter, and then return it to the earth in the spring either by burying it in your garden or by burning it and scattering the ashes over the earth.

The best corn dolls are those made from plants that have a significant place in your life. If you are not growing corn, see if there is some other plant in your garden that can be made into a corn doll. A friend of mine in Missouri earns part of her income by growing herbs and selling herbal products. She makes beautiful "corn dolls" out of southernwood, a species of *Artemisia*. Many plants, including the traditional grain plants, can be shaped, tied, and woven into dolls.

MIRROR, MIRROR, ON THE WALL

If you enjoy trance work, make your own scrying mirror. A mirror of this sort is used like any other reflective surface, and is easier to work with (and much less of a cliché) than a crystal ball. Many Pagans associate Hallowmas or Samhain with the art of divination, making that season a perfect time of year for putting together a scrying mirror.

The problem with ordinary mirrors is that they are *too* reflective. When you gaze into an ordinary mirror, you see yourself and your surroundings in a perfect, but reversed, reflection. That perfect reflection is usually a distraction, although there are plenty of anecdotal stories of people "seeing things" in normal mirrors. The theme is often used as a plot device in horror and fantasy stories.

For effective scrying, however, a less reflective mirror is more useful. An easy way to make a scrying mirror is to begin with an empty, off-the-rack picture frame like those sold at any discount or housewares store.

Remove the glass from the frame as if you were preparing to put a picture in it. Set the frame aside temporarily, then paint one side of the glass black. Apply the black paint evenly over the entire surface of the glass, leaving no visible streaks. Allow the paint to dry overnight.

The following day, place the glass back in the frame with the unpainted side facing out. You now have a scrying mirror!

Scrying is something a person experiences, not something a person learns intellectually. Sit in front of your mirror and try to clear your mind. It may help to turn off any electric lights and rely on one or two candles for illumination. Do not try to force anything; just gaze into the mirror and be open to any impressions you may receive. Some people describe a "clouding" effect just before they see images, so if the mirror clouds over, it probably means that you are starting to master this art.

If the mirror does not cloud over, do not worry; it may still work for you in a different way. Psychic impressions do not always manifest as visions (clairvoyance). Be open to anything that occurs as you gaze into the mirror. You may hear voices (clairaudience) or sense odors (clairalience). You may simply "know" things you did not know before (claircognizance).

Scrying mirrors make great presents for your Pagan friends. In fact, many of the things described in this chapter—scrying mirrors, personalized ritual candles, solar wreaths, sachets, and potpourri—can be assembled throughout the year as Yuletide presents, greatly reducing your shopping stress when December rolls around.

CHAPTER TEN

YULE

Yule is often confused with the winter solstice, but the former is a season while the latter is a precise moment in time. Yule begins with the Ærra Geola moon, which grows full in late November or the first few weeks of December, and the season then continues for two lunar months.

For Saxon Pagans (as well as Pagans from many other paths), the celebration of the Yuletide usually does not actually begin until Mothers' Night (the solstice) and continues for a week or two after this. I celebrate for twelve days, from Mothers' Night to New Year's Day, but I have been invited to Yule feasts held as late as mid-January. For that matter, I have attended Yule feasts that took place ten days or more *before* the solstice. And this was entirely appropriate, for Yule is a season.

I love Yule, partly because it is the most important holy tide in the Saxon sacral calendar, but also for the same reason that many non-Germanic Pagans love it. Wiccans have no reason to be exceptionally excited about the winter solstice, as it is a "minor sabbat" secondary to the big holidays like Beltane and Samhain. I have never known a Hellenic Pagan to make a big deal out of the Haloa, the December festival sacred to both Demeter and Dionysus, at least not more so than any other Greek festival. And yet Yule seems to have a special place in the hearts of most Pagans, regardless of their spiritual path, simply because it is so prevalent in our culture due to the influence of Christianity. The majority of first-generation Pagans (those of us who were raised by non-Pagan families) grew up in Christian households where we were introduced to Santa Claus, cinnamon cookies, eggnog, and jingle bells as children, and the oldest of us have passed these things on to our own children, the second- and third-generation Pagans of this century.

Although Pagans do not actually celebrate Christmas (as in "the birth of Christ"), we have no desire to relinquish the pleasantries of Christmas. Some Pagans claim that these traditions are ours, but any claim we may have to ownership is indirect at best.

While Christmas traditions may not literally be ours, the secular trappings of Christmas also have nothing to do with the birth of Jesus, and most of them suffer little or not at all when translated into a Pagan lifestyle. This is especially true for Pagans who follow Germanic paths, since so many of the Christmas customs we are familiar with originated in northern Europe. In my home we decorate a Yule tree each year. For us it represents the World Tree that connects all of the Seven Worlds. We enjoy munching on Yule cookies, and we have our favorite Yule songs. We do all of the secular things that our neighbors do, pretty much substituting the word *Yule* for the word *Christmas*.

Some people call this "stealing back," but I do not see where any theft is involved at all. These are the traditions of my ancestors, and while I follow a different religious path, my ancestors also chose to follow a path that differed from that of their own forebears; and none of this changes the fact that these are family traditions having little to do directly with either Jesus or Woden.

This is why I see nothing wrong or strange when non-Germanic Pagans also choose to celebrate Yule with evergreen trees, tinsel, and ho-ho-ho. These things have meaning to Pagans of all paths, and rightly so, because they are the ways of our ancestors.

It is in our spiritual expression where the diversity of this season manifests. As a Saxon Pagan, the birth of a Jewish boy more than two millennia ago has no special meaning for me. Nor do I believe that the sun is being "reborn." I do not celebrate the rites of Demeter and Dionysus. In short, I celebrate the season as a Saxon.

The winter solstice, for Saxons, is known as Módraniht, or Mothers' Night. This is the longest night of the year, and it is the night on which my kinsmen gather to offer a húsel to our female ancestors. It is believed that some mothers are very likely to care about their children, and their children's children, even after death. As the central part of the rite, a drinking horn is filled with mead, and we take turns drinking to the memory of our grandmothers, great-grandmothers, and great-great-grandmothers, back to the dawn of humankind. Many of us honor specific female ancestors by name. For us, it is the single most important night of the year, and it precedes a twelve-day celebration of the Yule.

Your Yuletide rituals should express your own spirituality. However much you may love "Christmas" traditions, it is important to remember that these are secular customs and not allow them to overshadow what the season means to you as a Pagan person.

Wassailing is one Yuletide tradition with a legitimate claim to a pre-Christian lineage (Simpson and Roud, p. 380). The word wassail comes from the Old English *wes hal*, meaning "be healthy" or "be whole," and is still often used even today as a salutation by Saxon Pagans. There were two traditional wassailing customs. One wassailing custom was associated with women and the other with men. Both included a warm, alcoholic drink often just called wassail.

The wassailing associated with women involved visiting neighbors' homes. A group of young women would carry a bowl of wassail from house to house. At each house they would offer wassail to the residents and sing a song. This was believed to bring luck to the household. The connection between this custom and the Pagan belief in female ancestors blessing their people on Mothers' Night is readily apparent.

This tradition is difficult to re-create today, since most if not all of your neighbors no longer honor their ancestors or the old gods. But the underlying purpose of wassailing like this was to celebrate the community or tribe, and that is very easy to re-create. When your coven or kindred is preparing to gather for a solstice celebration, find a selection of appropriate songs and print off the lyrics so everyone can sing along. These songs might be Pagan songs, but they can just as easily be secular carols. Set out a bowl of wassail, encourage everyone to take a cup, and then turn off the television. Instead of watching one more rerun of a Very Special Sugar-Coated Holiday Special, get everyone singing together, melding their voices and spirits in Pagan celebration.

The wassailing that was associated with men, also called "apple howling," was quite different. The men of the village would go to the local orchards and "wassail" the trees. This included singing to the trees and splashing the trunks with the wassail beverage. Specific practices varied from one village to the next. Toast soaked with wassail was sometimes placed in the tree branches. Here we have another tradition intended to bring luck, but this is luck for the orchards in the hope of a bountiful harvest in the coming year.

Apple howling is a great tradition to resurrect if you have planted even a single fruit- or nut-bearing tree in your yard. Pour some wassail around the roots of your tree (or trees), or put a slice of wassail-soaked toast in the branches. Sing to the tree. Here again the choice of song is entirely up to you. There might be a Pagan song you like; "The Trees of Annwfn" from Gwydion Pendderwen's 1982 album *The Faerie Shaman* would certainly be appropriate. Otherwise, you might choose a secular carol. I do not think the tree spirits really care what you sing. It is the attention they enjoy.

The traditional wassail beverage was a spiced ale or cider, and by "cider" I mean hard (alcoholic) cider. It was often described as "lamb's wool" because of the white froth on the surface of the drink. The following recipe is similar to what might have been used as wassail long ago. I say "similar" because the average Pagan in northern Europe obviously did not have access to sugar, ginger, or nutmeg.

TRADITIONAL WASSAIL

You will need:

    6 small apples

    1 ½ quarts ale or hard cider

    ¼ cup sugar

    1 teaspoon grated nutmeg

    1 teaspoon ground ginger

Preheat your oven to 120 degrees F. Core the apples and then place them on a lightly greased baking tray. The apples will swell slightly as they bake, so space them a couple inches apart from each other. Bake the apples for 1 hour.

Meanwhile, put 1 cup of the ale (or cider) and all of the sugar in a tall pan. Warm this over low heat, stirring continuously to dissolve the sugar. After the sugar has dissolved, add the grated nutmeg and ginger. Continue to simmer, stirring as you slowly add the remaining ale or cider.

After the apples are done baking, remove them from the oven and allow them to cool for 10 to 12 minutes. Then cut each apple in half and scoop out the baked "flesh" into a bowl. Discard the skins. (Ideally these apple skins should go into your compost!) Using a fork or potato masher, mash the apples until they are smooth.

Slowly add the smooth, mashed apples to the warm ale or cider, mixing them in vigorously with a whisk. Continue to warm the wassail over very low heat for about half an hour. Whisk again just before serving.

THOROUGHLY MODERN WASSAIL

One concern with a traditional wassail is that it is alcoholic. Much of the alcohol will dissipate as the wassail is heated, but it may still be unsuitable for some people. This next recipe is for a non-alcoholic wassail that all of your kinsmen can enjoy. You will need:

- 2 quarts apple juice or soft apple cider
- 2¼ cups pineapple juice
- 2 cups orange juice
- 1 cup lemon juice
- ½ cup sugar
- 1 stick cinnamon
- 1 teaspoon whole cloves

Put the cloves in a tea ball and mix all of these ingredients together in a pot. Warm the wassail over low heat. When it is heated through, remove the tea ball and serve the wassail in cups.

The Yule tree is usually a focal point in any solstice celebration if for no other reason than its physical size. Bringing an evergreen tree into the home at the solstice is a relatively modern custom, but there is nothing explicitly Christian about it (Israel is not notable for its vast pine forests), and as a Germanic tradition, it fits in very well with my Saxon spirituality. For me, the Yule tree represents the Eormensyl, the great Axis Mundi that touches each of the Seven Worlds.

Norse Pagans see the tree in a similar way: as Yggdrasil, connecting each of the Norse Nine Worlds.

The tree can become an expression of your spirituality even if you do not follow a northern path. The Hellenic (Greek) Pagan may want to decorate the tree with artificial grapes and either real or artificial vines in honor of the Haloa feast to Dionysus. The Roman Pagan with even marginal handicraft skills can incorporate the tree into a celebration of the Saturnalia. Make miniature scythes to hang from the tree branches (Saturnus is sometimes depicted holding a scythe), and include some solar ornaments in honor of Sol Invictus.

Assuming you already set up a Yule Tree every winter, or would like to do so in future, let us look at the essential nature of this practice. Those who purchase real trees can select from a variety of species, but all of the choices are evergreen trees. The other essential factor is that the tree, whether real or artificial, is always set up inside. You may also decide to put lights on evergreen trees outside the home, but the Yule tree itself is an indoor phenomenon.

Whether you set up a real tree (I hesitate to say "live tree" since technically it is dead as soon as it is cut) or an artificial tree is a matter of personal preference. Some people argue that it is better to buy an artificial tree than to kill a live tree, but, as with so many things, there are two sides to this issue. Very few trees brought into our homes at the solstice are wild trees pillaged from the forest. Almost all of them were planted, grown, and harvested for the express purpose of decorating our homes during the holidays. While they are growing, they do what all trees do, purifying and oxygenating the atmosphere. After the holidays, more than 90 percent of these trees are recycled through literally thousands of recycling programs. In contrast to this, artificial trees are non-recyclable and non-biodegradable, and they contribute absolutely nothing toward renewing our atmosphere.

I am not saying you are a bad person if you have decided to buy an artificial tree. What I am saying is that you are not a bad person if you have chosen a real tree.

The real tree has one other benefit: its needles. This may sound odd if you have ever cursed under your breath while picking dozens of stubborn evergreen needles out of a carpet, but those needles are wonderful as an aromatic ingredient for potpourri or incenses! After the holidays, before taking your tree out to be recycled, strip off the dry needles and store them in airtight containers away from light. Lay newspaper under the tree as you strip off the needles to catch everything that falls.

FOREST INCENSE

4 parts tree needles, broken up as small as possible

2 parts cedar shavings

1 part juniper berries, crushed

Blend these together for a delightful incense evoking the ambiance of deep woodlands. It is especially appropriate as incense for use in rituals honoring rural or forest deities. The scent will vary slightly depending on what species of tree you use, but the result is always pleasant.

To use this as a potpourri, add several drops of pine oil or juniper oil, and set the mixture out in an attractive bowl. The needles do not need to be broken up as finely.

At some point while shopping for Yuletide greenery you will undoubtedly come across those cute little rosemary herb topiaries shaped to resemble holiday trees. They are as irresistible as kittens, but I recommend you resist the urge to purchase one anyway. Rosemary is not a houseplant. Rosemary craves fresh air! It can (and must) be brought indoors before the first hard frost, but under the best conditions it can be difficult to keep alive through the winter. The rosemary topiary that looks so appealing at the store is not enjoying anything remotely resembling "best conditions." It has been stressed by trimming and has almost certainly received less than optimum care while waiting for someone to purchase it.

If a well-meaning friend gives you one of these herbs, the best you can do is hope to keep it alive until spring. Put the plant in a cool location that receives a lot of sunlight (yes, this is a contradiction; that is one reason why it is difficult to keep rosemary alive over the winter). Water the herb sparingly, keeping the soil fairly dry. Finally, mist the needles at least three or four times a week.

Then pray to whatever deity in your spiritual pantheon is sovereign over tender perennials. If your rosemary survives into the spring, get it outside as soon as the danger of a hard frost has passed.

If you live in a region that does not experience hard frosts, ignore everything I have just said. Enjoy your rosemary "tree" for a few days and then plant it outside where it can thrive.

What should you do with a dead rosemary plant? Maybe you could not resist the urge and bought a rosemary topiary despite my warning. Maybe a friend gave you a plant and you were (not surprisingly) unable to keep it alive until spring. Do the same thing as with an evergreen tree after the holidays: strip off the needles and use them as an aromatic. Rosemary needles make a wonderful incense, either alone or blended with other herbs.

What do you do on December 25th? For many people, there is no question about this. If you live in the same house or within a few miles of Christian relatives, it is very likely that they will want you to be with them as they commemorate the birth of their deity, and there is nothing wrong with that. You may have a job that requires you to work on the 25th, and there is nothing wrong with that either. But some of you may be in the same position I found myself in many years ago as I sat in my apartment with absolutely nothing to do. My Christian relatives all lived quite a distance from me, so that was not an obligation. My place of employment was closed, so going to work was not even an option. Cable television did not yet exist, nor did personal computers (to any extent), and I quickly discovered that my options in electronic entertainment were limited to a football game on one television channel and the Pope doing something or other on another channel.

After that, and for every year since then, December 25th at my home has been known as Gifting Day.

My híredmenn are always invited to Gifting Day, although there are no hard feelings if they have other obligations. In addition, other Pagan friends who do not have obligations to their careers or to blood kin are welcome to join us for a day of merriment and gift exchanging. There is an Anglo-Saxon style to our celebration. We always set out a large ham, for the boar was a sacred animal for our Saxon ancestors. The theme of the day is tribe and community; we already gave praise to our ancestors several days earlier, at the solstice.

I could leave December 25th to be an ordinary day, like any other day of the year, but why pass up an opportunity to make the most of a day when almost everyone I know has the day off work, and many have nothing else requiring their attention? And so I celebrate December 25th as Gifting Day, a day to celebrate my folk. The day becomes part of my sacral calendar. For me, it is also a time to give thanks for all of my friends and my híredmenn.

Earlier I mentioned that I celebrate the Yule for twelve days, but obviously Mothers' Night and Gifting Day are only two of those days. New Year's Eve is a third celebration. What about the other nine days?

For my inhíred, this varies from one year to the next. To ask what we do to celebrate the Yule is like asking where we each went on vacation; it is never the same thing from one year to the next. I like this flexibility, because every year our extended family is a little different. Work schedules change. Somebody enrolls in college or graduates from college. I may gain a new híredmann through marriage, or we may lose someone who moved away. One challenge for the twenty-first-century tribe is adapting to the demands of twenty-first-century life! We might gather for wassailing on one evening, or build a gingerbread house or hold a feast in honor of Sunne (the sovereign spirit of the sun), but what day we do any of this is different each year. On a day when most or all of us do not have to work, we will plan longer, more involved festivities.

Other Pagans, however, prefer a more structured schedule. Nick Egelhoff is a Norse Pagan who observes the twelve days of Yule with a series of devotionals. His household honors a different Norse deity or set of spirits each evening:

- December 20th: Mothers' Night. Offerings are given to the female ancestors, just as I would do. The Norse and the Saxons are both Germanic cultures, so we share quite a bit in common, although there are also many differences. In Nick's household, a libation of wine is also given to the Norse goddess Frigga on this solstice night.

- December 21st: Honoring Máni and the Wild Hunt. Máni, the Norse god of the moon, is praised and addressed as Brother of the Shining Sun. Offerings of beer, oatmeal, bread, and milk are given both to Máni and to Oðinn (Woden), who leads the Wild Hunt at this time of year.

- December 22nd: Sunna's Day. Offerings of incense and mead or wine are given to Sunna, the Norse goddess of the sun.

- December 23rd: Twins' Day. Offerings of beer, bread, and milk are given to Freyr and Freya, two deities known to Saxon Pagans as Ing and Fréo. This god and goddess are siblings associated with the prosperity or bounty of the earth.

- December 24th: Alfar's Night. The Alfar are a class of male ancestors that guard or watch over the inherited land of their descendants. Nick tells me that the Alfar "became conflated and connected with other types of spirits" in Norse culture, so they are at the same time ancestral spirits and land spirits. In Nick's household, the Alfar are given offerings of beer, bread, milk, or "anything that one's male ancestors might have enjoyed."

• December 25th: Children's Day. Nick and his wife do not yet have any children, but they believe it is important to honor children nevertheless on this day. "We remember and celebrate the innocence and joy of children," says Nick. Children's Day in his household is also a time to honor the spirits of hearth and home. Offerings—usually milk and cookies—are left out for the hausvættir (house elves).

• December 26th: Dvergar's Night. The dvergar are Norse dwarves. These spirits are believed to be excellent craftsmen. Nick honors them with offerings of jewelry, metals, and mead.

• December 27th: Forefathers' Day. Specific classes of ancestors are honored on Mothers' Night and Alfar's Night, but this day is devoted to all ancestors in a more general sense. As Nick puts it, the day is a time to honor the "nameless thousands whose blood, deeds, and luck flow within us." The offerings can be anything those ancestors might enjoy, but Nick often gives a libation of mead or some other fermented drink.

• December 28th: Hel's Night. In Germanic traditions, Hel is both a place and the goddess who reigns over that place. It is not a particularly bad place, nor is the goddess Hel (or Hella) a particularly bad goddess. Nick gives her offerings of mead, bread, and meat.

- December 29th: Ygg's Night. Ygg is another name for the god Oðinn, and this night is dedicated to him. The votive offering is always mead or some similar fermented drink, and Ygg is praised as the god who won the runic Mysteries.

- December 30th: Thunderer's Day. This day is dedicated to the god Thor, who is known to Saxon Pagans as Thunor. In Nick's devotional liturgy, he is addressed as "You who defend the Midgard, who are Friend to All Men, whose laughter sounds like the roll of thunder." Beer is the usual offering, but Nick tells me that he might also (or instead) give this god meat or bread.

- December 31st: Twelfth Night. On the last night of the year, Nick and his household honor the Norns, three powerful spirits who shape the fate of men. Fermented drink is the usual offering.

Obviously this is a much more structured approach to celebrating twelve days of Yule, and Nick admits it requires a willingness to adapt to worldly demands at times. This past year, he tells me, "We had to be flexible on one or two nights due to geography and timing. We traveled back to Columbus (Ohio) on Christmas Eve to be with my family, and thus we couldn't really do the devotionals as originally planned. But we made it work."

If you understand that plans may need to be changed, a structured twelve-day celebration may appeal more to you. This could be a series of twelve rituals, as Nick has done, or your tribe may want to alternate rituals with wassailing, feasting, or other Yuletide activities. The right way to do this is whatever way is both true to your spiritual tradition and fulfilling to you and your folk. When celebrating the twelve days of Yule, the important thing is not what you do or when you do it, so long as you do *something* throughout this twelve-day period of transition from one year to the next.

For those of us living in the Northern Hemisphere, the Yuletide brings another year to an end. And then a new year begins, unfolding before us as we walk a Pagan path.

GLOSSARY

Alfar: A class of male ancestors that guard or watch over the inherited land of their descendants. (Norse)

Ásatrú: Icelandic Paganism. This term is sometimes used in a more general way to include all Germanic paths, especially Scandinavian paths.

Beltane: A festival celebrated on or near the first of May, marking the beginning of summer. (Irish Celtic, Wiccan)

blót: A sacrifice to the gods or ancestors. The word literally means "blood," but Norse Pagans generally use the term for any offering. (Norse, Saxon)

Calan Awst: A festival celebrated on or near the first of August, marking the beginning of the harvest season. (Welsh Celtic)

demos: A name used by many Hellenic Pagans for the tribe or spiritual family. Plural, *demoi.* (Hellenic)

Dodekatheon: The twelve Olympic gods and goddesses of the Hellenic Pantheon. (Hellenic) *dvergar:* An Old Norse word for dwarves—subterranean spirits associated with metals and gems, craftsmanship and wisdom. (Norse)

Eormensyl: The Axis Mundi that connects the Seven Worlds of Anglo-Saxon cosmology. Sometimes called the World Tree. (Saxon)

esbat: A coven meeting that takes place at some time other than one of the sabbats. Esbats are usually held on or near the full moon. (Wiccan)

Gallic: Coming from or originating in Gaul, a region of Europe that corresponds roughly to the modern nation of France. Gallic Pagans revere continental Celtic deities such as Taranis, Ogmios, and Lugus.

gesith: An oathed member of an inhíred, sworn to brotherhood. The word literally means "comrade" or "companion." Plural, *gesithas.* (Saxon)

Hal Sidu: Old English for "healthy (hale) custom." Holistic traditions that bring together the body, mind, and spirit.

hama: The astral body that surrounds and protects the physical self. As a proper noun, this is also the name of the god known to the Norse as Heimdall. (Saxon)

hausvættir: Another term for house elves. (Norse)

Hellenic: Relating to the ancient Greeks. Hellenic Pagans revere the deities of the Dodekatheon with reconstructions of ancient Greek ritual.

hiredmann: Any member of an inhíred, oathed or not. Plural, *hiredmenn.* (Saxon)

húsel: A sacrifice to the gods or ancestors. (Saxon)

Imbolc: A festival celebrated on or near the first of February, marking the beginning of spring. It is associated with the lactation of ewes in early spring. (Irish Celtic, Wiccan)

inhíred: The tribe or extended family. The name means "household." Plural, *inhírdas.* (Saxon)

Kemetic: Relating to the ancient Egyptians. Kemetic Pagans revere deities such as Isis, Osiris, and Horus with reconstructions of Egyptian ritual.

kindred: The tribe or extended family. (Norse)

Lammas: A festival celebrated on or near the first of August, celebrating the bread baked from the first wheat harvest. (Saxon, Wiccan)

lararium: A household altar. Literally, the dwelling place of the household guardian spirits. (Roman)

Lughnasadh: A festival celebrated on or near the first of August to commemorate the goddess Tailtiu, foster mother of Lugh. Like Lammas and Calan Awst, this is a harvest festival. (Irish Celtic, Wiccan)

Midgard: The physical world. Middle Earth, in contrast to the extradimensional worlds that surround the physical universe in Germanic cosmology. (Norse)

Midsummer: The summer solstice. (Saxon, Wiccan)

Módraniht: Mothers' Night, the winter solstice. The longest night of the year is a time to honor one's female ancestors (foremothers) with libations and praise. (Saxon)

myse: The working surface for magical or spiritual rituals. The name means "table" in Old English. (Saxon)

Neo-Pagans: A term referring to contemporary, living Pagan people. Neo-Pagans follow a wide array of spiritual paths.

numina: A word meaning "powers," sometimes used in reference to guardian spirits. (Roman)

Paleo-Pagans: A term referring to Pagan people who lived in pre-Christian cultures, in contrast to modern Neo-Pagans.

recelsfæt: A censer. Any container for holding burning incense. (Saxon)

Saxon: Relating to the Germanic tribes who settled in England from the third century onward. Saxon Pagans revere deities such as Woden, Frige, and Thunor with reconstructions of Anglo-Saxon ritual.

spelt: A variety of wheat that was a staple crop from the Bronze Age to the Middle Ages. Often favored by Roman and Hellenic Pagans for use as an offering.

wéofod: An altar. Literally, the place where the image of the deity stands. (Saxon)

wéofodsteall: Shrine or sacred ritual space. Literally, the place where the altar is. (Saxon)

wéoh: An image or symbol of a deity. An idol. (Saxon)

Ygg: One of the many names of the god Oðinn. (Norse)

BIBLIOGRAPHY

Albertsson, Alaric. *Travels Through Middle Earth: The Path of a Saxon Pagan*. Woodbury, MN: Llewellyn Publications, 2009.

———. *Wyrdworking: The Path of a Saxon Sorcerer*. Woodbury, MN: Llewellyn Publications, 2011.

Ambrose, J. T., et al. *The Hive and the Honeybee*. Revised edition. Hamilton, IL: Dadant & Sons, 1992.

Andrews, Ted. *Animal-Speak*. St. Paul, MN: Llewellyn Publications, 1993.

Bartholomew, Mel. *Square Foot Gardening*. Emmaus, PA: Rodale Press, 1981.

Beyerl, Paul. *The Master Book of Herbalism*. Custer, WA: Phoenix Publishing, 1984.

Blake, Deborah. *Everyday Witch Book of Rituals*. Woodbury, MN: Llewellyn Publications, 2012.

Bremness, Lesley. *The Complete Book of Herbs*. New York: Viking Studio Books, 1988.

Briggs, Katharine. *An Encyclopedia of Fairies*. New York: Pantheon Books, 1976.

Burkert, Walter. *Greek Religion*. Translated by John Raffan. Malden, MA: Blackwell Publishing, 1985.

Cunningham, Scott. *Magical Herbalism*. St. Paul, MN: Lewellyn Publications, 1982.

Dennis, John V. *The Wildlife Gardener*. New York: Alfred A. Knopf, 1985.

Findhorn Community, The. *The Findhorn Garden: Pioneering a New Vision of Man and Nature in Cooperation*. New York: Harper Colophon Books, 1975.

Griffiths, Bill. *Aspects of Anglo-Saxon Magic*. Norfolk, UK: Anglo-Saxon Books, 1996.

Guirand, Felix, ed. *Larousse Encyclopedia of Mythology*. New York: Prometheus Press, 1959.

Hartley, Dorothy. *Lost Country Life*. New York: Pantheon Books, 1979.

Jones, Prudence, and Nigel Pennick. *A History of Pagan Europe*. New York: Routledge, 1995.

Kilarski, Barbara. *Keep Chickens!: Tending Small Flocks in Cities, Suburbs, and Other Small Spaces*. North Adams, MA: Storey Publishing, 2003.

Langer, Richard W. *Grow It!* New York: Avon Books, 1972.

Murray, Elizabeth. *Cultivating Sacred Space: Gardening for the Soul*. San Francisco: Pomegranate, 1997.

Murray, Margaret A. *The God of the Witches*. New York: Oxford University Press, 1952.

Olkowski, Helga and William. *The City People's Book of Raising Food*. Emmaus, PA: Rodale Press, 1975.

Pitcairn, Richard H., DVM, and Susan Hubble Pitcairn. *Dr. Pitcairn's Complete Guide to Natural Health for Dogs and Cats.* Emmaus, PA: Rodale Press, 1982.

Riotte, Louise. *Planetary Planting.* New York: Simon & Schuster, 1975.

Schwanz, Lee, ed. *The Family Poultry Flock.* Brookfield, WI: Farmer's Digest, 1979.

Simpson, Jacqueline, and Steve Roud. *A Dictionary of English Folklore.* Oxford, UK: Oxford University Press, 2000.

Trout, Darrell. *Kitchen Garden Planner.* Des Moines, IA: Country Home Books, 1999.

INDEX

TO WRITE TO THE AUTHOR

If you wish to contact the author or would like more information about this book, please write to the author in care of Llewellyn Worldwide Ltd. and we will forward your request. Both the author and publisher appreciate hearing from you and learning of your enjoyment of this book and how it has helped you. Llewellyn Worldwide Ltd. cannot guarantee that every letter written to the author can be answered, but all will be forwarded. Please write to:

Alaric Albertsson
% Llewellyn Worldwide
2143 Wooddale Drive
Woodbury, MN 55125-2989

Please enclose a self-addressed stamped envelope for reply, or $1.00 to cover costs. If outside the U.S.A., enclose an international postal reply coupon.